The Conconully Mining District of Okanogan County, Washington

Washington Geological Survey

with an introduction by Kerby Jackson

Introduction

It has been over forty years since the Washington Geological Survey released it's important publication "Conconcully Mining District of Okanogan County, Washington". First released in 1973, this important volume has been out of print and has been unavailable to the mining community since those days, with the exception of expensive original collector's copies and poorly produced digital editions.

It has often been said that "*gold is where you find it*", but even beginning prospectors understand that their chances for finding something of value in the earth or in the streams of the Golden West are dramatically increased by going back to those places where gold and other minerals were once mined by our forerunners. Despite this, much of the contemporary information on local mining history that is currently available is mostly a result of mere local folklore and persistent rumors of major strikes, the details and facts of which, have long been distorted. Long gone are the old timers and with them, the days of first hand knowledge of the mines of the area and how they operated. Also long gone are most of their notes, their assay reports, their mine maps and personal scrapbooks, along with most of the surveys and reports that were performed for them by private and government geologists. Even published books such as this one are often retired to the local landfill or backyard burn pile by the descendents of those old timers and disappear at an alarming rate. Despite the fact that we live in the so-called "Information Age" where information is supposedly only the push of a button on a keyboard away, true insight into mining properties remains illusive and hard to come by, even to those of us who seek out this sort of information as if our lives depend upon it. Without this type of information readily available to the average independent miner, there is little hope that our metal mining industry will ever recover.

This important volume and others like it, are being presented in their entirety again, in the hope that the average prospector will no longer stumble through the overgrown hills and the tailing strewn creeks without being well informed enough to have a chance to succeed at his ventures.

Kerby Jackson
Josephine County, Oregon
January 2015

CONTENTS

	Page
Preface	III
Introduction	1
Location and physiography	1
Distribution of mineral deposits	1
Previous work	2
Mining history	3
Production	7
Conconully area	7
Geology	7
Ore deposits	9
Principal mines	10
Arlington	10
Fourth of July	13
Sonny Boy	14
First Thought	16
Last Chance	17
Nevada (War Eagle-Peacock)	18
Wheeler (Mineral Hill)	20
Mohawk	24
Lone Star	24
Miscellaneous mines and prospects	26
Ruby Hill-Peacock Mountain area	26
Woo Loo Moo Loo prospect	26
Keystone prospect	27
Hughes prospect	27
Plant-Callahan mine	27
Johnny Boy prospect	27
Mineral Hill area	27
Leuena mine	27
Conconully-Salmon Creek area	27
Gubser prospect	27
John Arthur prospect	28
Tough Nut mine	28
Homestake mine	28
Key mine	28

Conconully area—Continued

    Miscellaneous mines and prospects—Continued

        Conconully-Salmon Creek area—Continued

                Monitor mine 28

                Salmon River prospect 29

                Copper King prospect 29

                Esther prospect 29

                Lady of the Lake prospect 29

                Silver King mine 29

Blue Lake area 33

                Gold Quarry prospect 33

                Okanogan Copper prospect 33

                Blue Lake mine 33

                Q. S. prospect 34

Galena area 34

                Silver Bluff mine 34

                Silver Bell prospect 34

                Eureka prospect 34

                Lulu prospect 34

                Black Huzzar prospect 35

                Belcher prospect 35

Isolated occurrences 35

                Carl Frederick (Bernhardt) prospect 35

                Starr mine 35

                Central (Trinidad) mine 37

                Tonasket (Montgomery) prospect 38

                Sherman mine 38

                Buck Mountain (Buckhorn) mine 39

Outlook for the district 40

Selected references 41

ILLUSTRATIONS

Page

Figure 1. Index map showing location of Conconully mining district 2

2. Mining camps (1887) and general location of the patented mining
claims of the Conconully area 4

3. General geology and mines and prospects of the Conconully area 8

4. Arlington mine workings 11

5. Fourth of July mine workings 14

6. Sonny Boy mine workings 15

7. First Thought and Last Chance claim map 17

8. Nevada claim map and mine workings 19

9. Wheeler mine claim map and mine workings 21

10. Mohawk mine workings 23

11. Lone Star claim map and mine workings 25

12. Patented mining claims of the Conconully area 30

13. Patented mining claims of the Ruby Hill area 31

14. General geology and mines and prospects of the Blue Lake area 32

15. Starr mine workings 36

16. Sherman mine claim map 39

CONCONULLY MINING DISTRICT

of

OKANOGAN COUNTY, WASHINGTON

By Wayne S. Moen

INTRODUCTION

LOCATION AND PHYSIOGRAPHY

The Conconully mining district of central Okanogan County encompasses 525 square miles of the Okanogan Highlands physiographic province of Washington. The district falls within Township 34 North through Township 37 North, and extends westward from the Okanogan River to the middle of Range 23 East (fig. 1).

The topography of the district consists of gently rolling grassy range lands in the east half, and moderately to heavily timbered mountainous lands in the west half; many parts of the mountainous areas are steep and rocky. Along the Okanogan River elevations range from 850 to 900 feet; however, they increase rapidly westward to a maximum of 8,242 feet on the summit of Tiffany Mountain, which is in the northwest corner of the district. In the vicinity of Conconully, the average elevation is 3,600 feet.

Numerous streams, both permanent and intermittent, form a dendritic drainage pattern in the district. Salmon Creek, which is the largest stream, has its headwaters in the northwest part of the district, and joins the Okanogan River near Okanogan in the southeast corner of the district. Other main creeks include the Sinlahekin and Loup Loup. Many lakes are to be found in the east half of the district; the largest are Conconully, Fish, and Blue.

DISTRIBUTION OF MINERAL DEPOSITS

Most mineral deposits of the Conconully mining district occur in the central part of the district, and within 7 miles of Conconully (fig. 1). The deposits of the Conconully area contain mainly silver, lead, and copper; however, minor amounts of gold, zinc, and molybdenum are also present.

In the Blue Lake area, which is 8 miles north of Conconully, several veins contain sparsely disseminated copper minerals and gold. In the Galena area, which is 6 miles east of Conconully, several deposits contain silver and copper.

Elsewhere in the district, isolated mineral occurrences contain molybdenum,

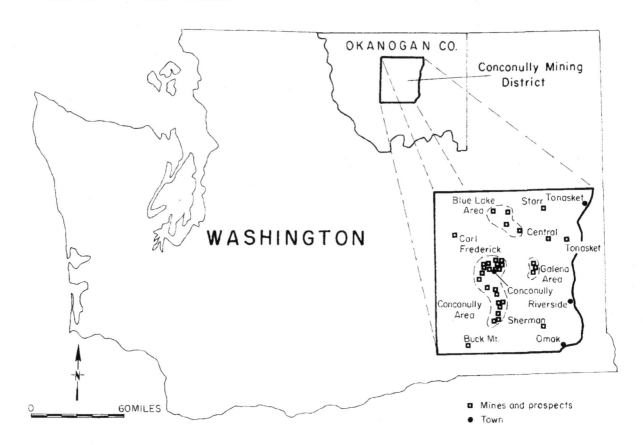

FIGURE 1.—Index map showing location of Conconully mining district.

tungsten, copper, lead, zinc, gold, and silver.

PREVIOUS WORK

The earliest account of the mineral occurrences of the Conconully mining district was given in 1891 by George A. Bethune, who was the first State Geologist. In his first annual report on the mines and minerals of Washington, Bethune proclaimed the Conconully mining district as one of the most promising in the state. In 1897, L. K. Hodges prepared a report for the Seattle Post-intelligencer titled "Mining in the Pacific Northwest." A history of the district, as well as a discussion on the mines and prospects that were active in the late 1890's, appears in Hodges' report. In 1916, Edward L. Jones, Jr., reported on the district in U.S. Geological Survey Bulletin No. 640-B, "Reconnaissance of the Conconully and Ruby Mining Districts, Washington." Jones' report covers mines and prospects that were active in the early 1900's, metallurgic investigations of the district's ores, and the geology of the area.

In unpublished theses, the geology of the Conconully area has been mapped by Richard Goldsmith (1952) and F. J. Menzer (1964). Goldsmith reports on the petrology of the Tiffany-Conconully area, while Menzer discusses the geology of the crystalline rocks west of Okanogan, which includes the Ruby Hill area.

MINING HISTORY

Prior to 1886, Okanogan County west of the Okanogan River was part of the Chief Moses Indian Reservation. Although mineral deposits were known to be present on the reservation, it was not until the spring of 1886, when the reservation was opened to mineral entry, that the deposits could be legally staked as mining claims. When the reservation was opened, prospectors rushed to the area near Conconully Lake and staked claims on deposits rich in lead and silver. One of the first discoveries was the Lady of the Lake that was staked by George Runnels on May 10, 1886, on the north shore of Conconully Lake. One mile north of Runnels' discovery, the John Arthur, Lone Star, Tough Nut, and other important discoveries were staked. In the vicinity of Conconully Lake, prospectors organized the Salmon River mining district, while several miles to the northeast the Galena district was organized. At the present site of Conconully, the mining camp of Salmon City was established. In the fall of 1886, rich deposits of silver were discovered 6 miles south of Salmon City on Ruby Hill. Among

the first claims to be staked were the Ruby, Poorman, First Thought, and Second Thought. In the spring of 1887, the Arlington and Fourth of July veins were discovered, which resulted in the organization of the Ruby Hill mining district. West of the discoveries on Ruby Hill, Loup Loup City sprang up, while east of Ruby Hill, on Salmon Creek, Ruby City came into existence (fig. 2).

By 1889, several hundred mining claims had been staked in the Salmon River, Galena, and Ruby mining districts; silver ore was mined and stockpiled at many mines awaiting shipment to distant smelters. In December 1889, silver-rich lead ore was shipped from the Monitor mine to a Montana smelter. Shortly thereafter, high-grade silver ore from the Fourth of July mine on Ruby Hill was also shipped to Montana for smelting, and a profit of several hundred dollars per ton was realized. Following these initial shipments, silver ore left monthly from the mines of the district for smelters as far away as Denver and San Francisco. However, transportation of the ore proved to be costly. From Conconully, it was a 45-mile wagon haul to Brewster; from Brewster, river boats transported the ore 80 miles down the Columbia River to Wenatchee. From Wenatchee, the ore was shipped by rail to smelters, some of which were many hundred miles away.

Inasmuch as only the richest ores could be shipped profitably to distant smelters, several concentrating plants were erected in the district to treat low-grade silver ore. The largest concentrating plant was built at

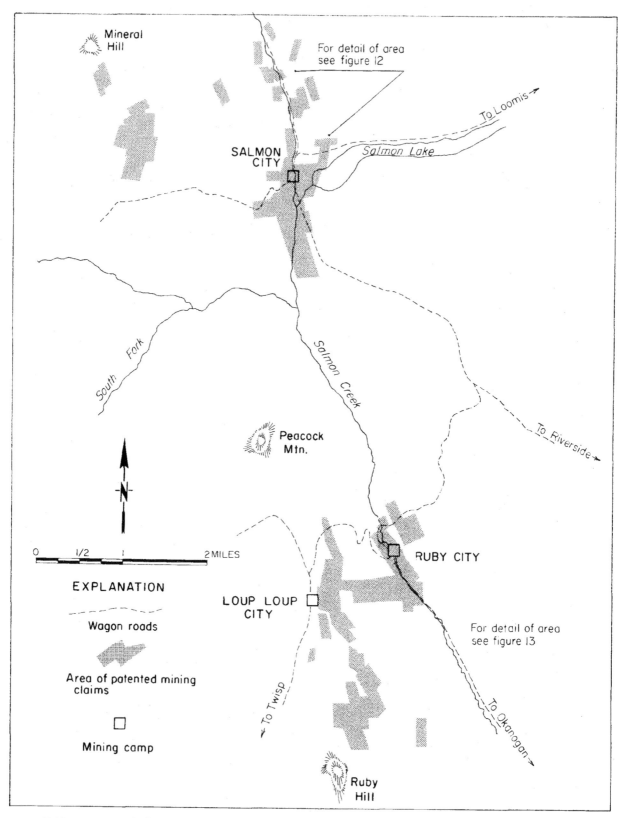

FIGURE 2.—*Mining camps (1887) and general location of the patented mining claims of the Conconully area.*

Ruby City by Washington Reduction Company in 1892. The company also built a 1½-mile-long aerial tram from its mill to the First Thought mine on Ruby Hill. Between October 1892 and June 1893, silver ore from the First Thought, as well as from the Last Chance, Arlington, and Fourth of July mines, was treated at the Ruby City concentrator. Prior to building the concentrating mill at Ruby City, Arlington Mining Company started construction of a large mill, 1 mile southwest of the Arlington mine and several hundred feet east of Loup Loup Creek. However, because of an inadequate supply of water the mill was never finished. Hidden amongst the pine trees, the massive granite-block foundation walls still stand as a monument to the early miners on Ruby Hill. The concentrating mills that were built elsewhere in the districts were doomed to failure when it was found that they were improperly designed to treat the silver ores. However, hand-sorted ores could still be shipped at a profit. Small shipments of high-grade silver ore were made from the Mohawk, Levena, and Columbia mines on Mineral Hill, and from the Tough Nut mine on Salmon Creek, north of Conconully.

In 1893, the price of silver fell to 90 cents per ounce, and it was no longer profitable to work the mines. The mining camps of Loup Loup City and Ruby City became deserted, and the concentrating mill at Ruby City shut down; however, Salmon City, which had changed its name to Conconully in 1888, managed to survive because, in addition to being a mining center, it had grown into an active farming community.

Following the silver panic of 1893, little in the way of silver mining was undertaken in the silver camps of Washington until 1900. In the Conconully area, mining resumed at the Columbia mine in 1901, and at the Arlington mine in 1905. However, mining operations at both mines ceased by 1906.

Around 1915, two attempts were made to explore the silver-bearing veins of the Conconully area at depths of up to 1,000 feet beneath the surface. From the west bank of Salmon Creek, about one-half mile north of Ruby City, Peacock Mining and Milling Company started a crosscut westerly into Peacock Mountain for the purpose of intersecting, at depth, the many veins that cropped out on the mountain. After completing only 700 feet of the proposed 2,100-foot crosscut, the project was terminated. One mile north of Conconully on the west bank of Salmon Creek, Washington Consolidated Mines & Reduction Company started a crosscut westerly into Mineral Hill for the purpose of developing silver-bearing veins that had proven to be rich on the surface. After completing 875 feet of the proposed 10,000-foot crosscut, the project was abandoned.

In the early 1920's, mining was once again undertaken at the Arlington, First Thought, and Last Chance mines. Several shipments of ore were made to smelters, but because of high freight costs, once again it proved unprofitable to ship low-grade crude ore, and the mines shut down. However, in 1936 a concentrating mill was built at the Arlington mine, and the mill produced copper and silver concentrate from Arlington ore until 1940. Small concentrating mills were built at the Sonny Boy and Columbia mines in 1939, and small shipments of lead, silver, and copper concentrates were made from both mines until 1946.

Between 1947 and 1950, most of the work in the district was of the assessment nature. In 1951, mining of lead-silver ore began at the Mohawk mine on Mineral Hill, and continued through 1954. At the Nevada mine on Peacock Mountain, mining began in 1954, and continued through 1957. In 1958, after having been shut down for 60 years, silver ore was shipped from the Fourth of July mine on Ruby Hill; shipments from the mine continued through 1964.

Since 1964, only exploration and development work has been undertaken at the silver mines of the Conconully area. Much of the work was done by Sunny Peak Mining Company at deposits on Mineral Hill. In 1972, Silver Consolidated Mining Company of Spokane rehabilitated mine workings at the Mohawk and Nevada mines for the purpose of placing the mines into production.

In other parts of the Conconully mining district, many claims were staked following the initial discoveries in the Conconully area; however, most of the claims were abandoned when the prospectors found that the veins were only sparsely metallized. Small shipments of ore were made from a few isolated occurrences, but no property became a major producer.

Six miles east of Conconully, in an area that prior to 1900 was known as the Galena mining district, deposits of copper and silver were explored in the late 1800's and early 1900's. The only production from this area came from the Silver Bluff mine, which produced $80,000 in copper and silver by the end of 1923.

The discoveries of gold and copper, which had been made in the Blue Lake area in the late 1800's, proved to contain low-grade ore. The only production from the area came from the Blue Lake mine, which, in 1901, produced 5,000 tons of ore.

In the Tiffany Mountain area, which is in the northwestern corner of the district, argentiferous galena was discovered by C. Bernhard in 1906. Exploratory work was carried out at the property until the late 1920's, but shipments of ore were never made.

West of Tonasket, on the east flank of Aeneas Mountain, molybdenum was discovered in 1915 by Andrew Starr. The deposit was extensively explored in 1928, 1935, and 1936. The Starr mine never developed into a major producer, although a 3,000-ton shipment of molybdenum was made in 1939. Exploration work continues to be carried out at the mine. As recently as 1970, core drilling was undertaken, and in 1972 geochemical and geophysical surveys were being made.

Several miles southwest of Tonasket, in the vicinity of Turtle Lake, veins containing gold, silver, copper, and lead were discovered around 1915. The metals were sparse, and the only production from the area was in 1918, when the Central mine shipped 30 tons of low-grade gold and silver ore.

In the Omak area, deposits of gold, silver, lead, and zinc were discovered by Ezra Sherman in 1916. Several hundred tons of ore was produced in 1958, and since 1960, Sherman Mining Company has been actively exploring the deposits.

PRODUCTION

Because of incomplete production records for the Conconully mining district, it is impossible to determine with any accuracy the value of metals mined in the district. A fairly conservative figure for lead, silver, copper, and gold production is around $350,000. The most productive years were from 1889 through 1893, when the combined silver production from the Arlington, First Thought, Last Chance, and Fourth of July mines totaled $200,000. The next most productive years were 1937 through 1939, when the Arlington mine shipped silver-copper concentrates that had a net value of $71,683. The last production for the district was from 1958 through 1964, when silver ore worth around $12,000 was shipped from the Fourth of July mine. The district's remaining production is distributed among eight other mines, most of which made small shipments of high-grade silver ore prior to 1900.

CONCONULLY AREA

GEOLOGY

In the Conconully area, which contains the majority of the district's mineral deposits, the predominant rocks are granodiorite, migmatite, schist, and gneiss (fig. 3).

The granodiorite occurs mainly in the west half of the area, and is separated from schists and gneisses of the eastern half by sharp intrusive contacts, transitional zones of migmatitic rocks, and steeply dipping faults. The granodiorite is part of the Similkameen batholith of western Okanogan County. The schists and gneisses are a small part of a metamorphosed sequence that underlies large areas of central Okanogan County.

West of Conconully, on Mineral Hill, hornblende granodiorite, biotite granodiorite, and porphyritic granodiorite have been mapped by Goldsmith (1952) as Mineral Hill granodiorite. South of Conconully, on Little Peacock Mountain and Ruby Hill, biotite granodiorite, porphyritic granodiorite, quartz diorite, and quartz monzonite have been mapped by Menzer (1964) as Loup Loup granodiorite. The granodiorite, as well as some of the metamorphic rocks, contain dikelike and irregular masses of aplite and pegmatite. Although most aplites and pegmatites are void of ore minerals, a pegmatitic dike in the Wheeler mine on Mineral Hill contains sparsely disseminated grains of molybdenite. The granodiorite, as well as some migmatites, also contains small, dark dikes that resemble amphibolite or lamprophyre; the dikes are not known to contain ore minerals.

The gneisses and schists of the area have been mapped by Goldsmith and Menzer as Salmon Creek schists and gneisses. They consist of pelitic quartzitic schist, mica schist, amphibolitic schist, calc-silicate

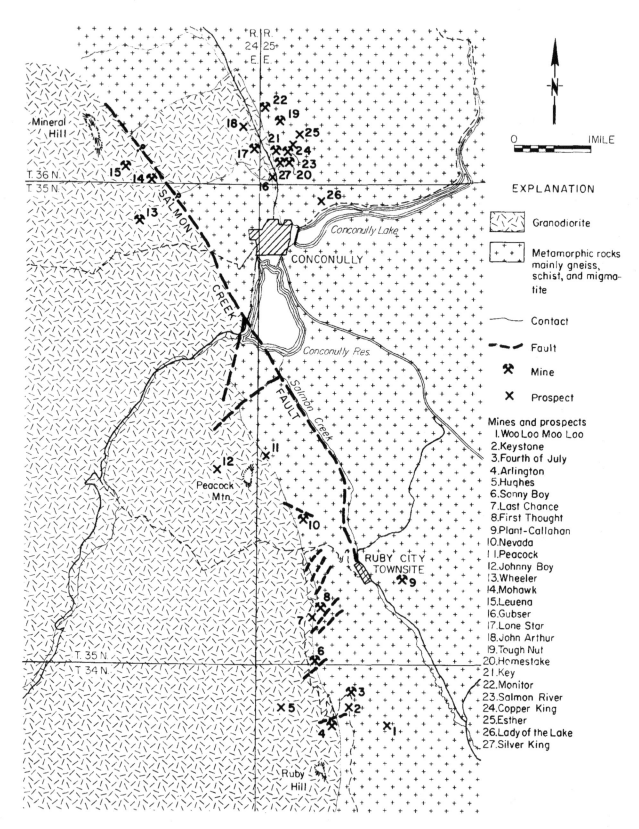

EXPLANATION

Granodiorite

Metamorphic rocks mainly gneiss, schist, and migmatite

Contact

Fault

Mine

Prospect

Mines and prospects
1. Woo Loo Moo Loo
2. Keystone
3. Fourth of July
4. Arlington
5. Hughes
6. Sonny Boy
7. Last Chance
8. First Thought
9. Plant-Callahan
10. Nevada
11. Peacock
12. Johnny Boy
13. Wheeler
14. Mohawk
15. Leuena
16. Gubser
17. Lone Star
18. John Arthur
19. Tough Nut
20. Homestake
21. Key
22. Monitor
23. Salmon River
24. Copper King
25. Esther
26. Lady of the Lake
27. Silver King

FIGURE 3.—General geology and mines and prospects of the Conconully area.

quartzite, calc-silicate marble, quartz diorite gneiss, gneissose lime-silicate, granulite, and amphibolite. The metamorphic rocks were derived from Paleozoic sediments and volcanics that were subjected to regional metamorphism during the Jurassic orogeny, and which were later invaded by granitic magmas of probably late Mesozoic age.

The contact between the granodiorite and metamorphic rocks has a general northwest trend, and parallels the regional structural trend of the metamorphic rocks of the area. On Mineral Hill the contact is sharp and of an intrusive nature; along parts of the contact, dikelike bodies of granodiorite project into the metamorphic rocks. On Little Peacock Mountain and Ruby Hill, the contact for the most part is gradational and consists of migmatitic gneiss. Near Conconully, the granodiorite is separated from the metamorphic rocks by a steeply dipping northwest-trending fault of unknown displacement. On Ruby Hill, several high-angle faults obliquely cut the contact zone, which contains several metallized quartz veins, and offset the zone from 6 to 10 feet.

ORE DEPOSITS

Most of the lead, silver, and copper deposits of the Conconully area consist of quartz fissure veins that occur adjacent to the contact zone between granodiorite and metamorphic rocks (fig. 3). Although quartz veins may be found throughout the area, those that contain significant concentrations of ore minerals appear to fall within three distinct areas. The southern area, which has been the most productive area to date, is on Ruby Hill. The northern area is one-half to $1\frac{1}{2}$ miles north of Conconully and contains at least 11 deposits. The third area is on the southern slope of Mineral Hill, $1\frac{1}{2}$ miles west of Conconully. In this area the deposits are as much as 1 mile from the contact zone.

The quartz veins of the Conconully area range from thin stringers less than 1 inch in thickness to massive veins that are as much as 20 feet in thickness, averaging from 3 to 6 feet. The veins exhibit a wide variety of strikes ranging from N. 55° E. through N. 50° W., with the average strike being about N. 10° W. The dips of the veins are from 25° to 90° east and west, and average about 60° to 70°. In several mines, the veins have been followed for 500 to 600 feet along their strikes and dips.

The ore minerals of the veins, in order of decreasing abundance, are galena, tetrahedrite, chalcopyrite, bornite, and sphalerite. Pyrite is almost always present in the veins; however, it is more abundant in the part of the vein that contains ore minerals. In most veins the ore minerals are concentrated into bands and lenses, 6 to 40 inches thick, that parallel the walls of the veins. The bands and lenses are usually discontinuous in the veins and vary in length from a few feet to as much as 200 feet, along both the strike and dip of the veins. Sections of the veins between the bands and lenses of ore minerals usually consist of barren quartz.

Silver is the most valuable metal in the veins and occurs mainly in the tetrahedrite. Bethune (1892, p. 86) reported that selected samples of tetrahedrite from the First Thought mine contained as much as 1,926 ounces of silver per ton. Jones (1916, p. 23) states that minerals from the Key mine contained silver as follows:

Mineral	Silver (ounces/ton)
Tetrahetrite	347.6
Galena	71.1
Sphalerite	29.5
Pyrite	26.4
Quartz	None

Early reports on the mines of the Conconully area state that near-surface parts of some veins contained ore that assayed over 1,000 ounces per ton in silver, and hand-sorted ore assayed as much as 450 ounces of silver per ton for carload lots that were shipped to smelters. However, ore that was concentrated at concentrating mills in the district contained around 50 ounces of silver per ton. The lead content of the veins ranged from 1 to 10 percent; the average silver ore that was mined contained around 3.5 percent lead. The copper content averaged 1.5 percent, and the average gold content was 0.03 ounce.

The vertical extent of the ore minerals appears to be as much as 2,500 feet in the Mineral Hill-Salmon Creek area, and 1,500 feet on Ruby Hill. Near the surface, oxidation is only slight; for the most part, primary ore minerals extend to the surface. Secondary enrichment does not appear to be present. Near-surface parts of the veins tend to be rich in tetrahedrite. As depths increase, galena and sphalerite predominate. At deeper depths, these minerals give way to chalcopyrite and bornite, and finally pyrrhotite.

The formation of the metallized quartz veins of the Conconully area is believed to be the result of the following factors:

1. Fracturing along the borders of a crystallizing granodioritic magma, the fractures being localized to some extent by the relative competency of the granodiorite, gneiss, schist, and migmatite.

2. Residual silica from the magma was injected into fractures and formed quartz veins.

3. Adjustments in the contracting and cooling magma caused further fracturing, which sheared the brittle quartz and permitted metal-bearing hydrothermal solutions to enter and precipitate out as ore minerals.

4. Recurrent movement along the veins granulated some ore minerals and drew them out into long thin bands.

PRINCIPAL MINES

For the purpose of this report, the principal mines of the Conconully area are mines that have in the past been major silver producers, or mines that may become silver producers in the future because of higher silver prices. Other mines of the Conconully area may be equally as important; however, the writer does not have sufficient data at this time to properly discuss them.

Arlington

The Arlington mine, which has been the major silver producer of the area, is 4 miles by road from the old Ruby City townsite on Salmon Creek. The main workings of the

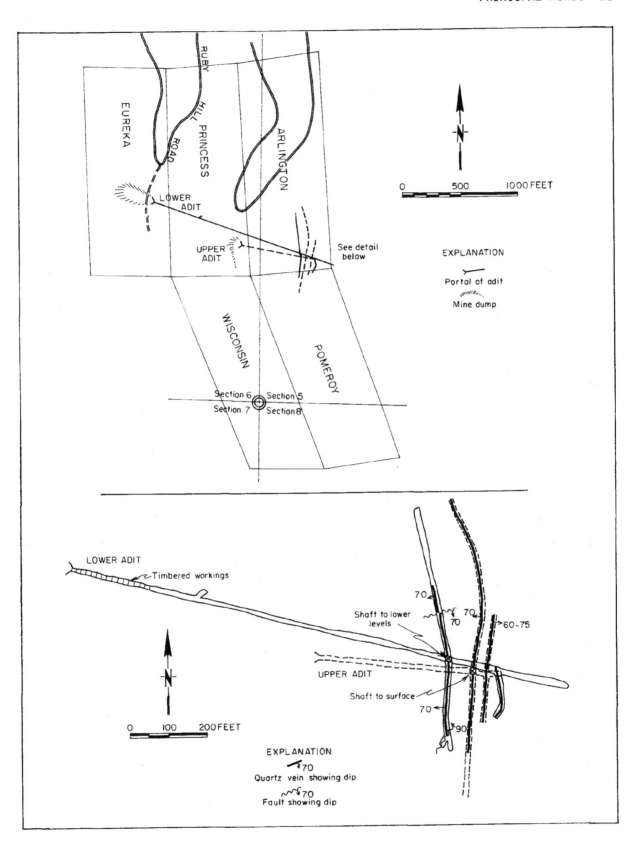

FIGURE 4.—Arlington mine workings.

mine are covered by nine patented and three unpatented mining claims that are on the northwestern slope of Ruby Hill in the NE$\frac{1}{4}$SE$\frac{1}{4}$ sec. 6, T. 34 N., R. 25 E., at an elevation of 4,080 feet. Currently the mine is idle, and the main adit is caved at its portal, which makes most of the mine workings inaccessible.

The Arlington vein, which was one of the first to be discovered on Ruby Hill, was staked in the fall of 1887 by John Oleson. The Arlington Mining Company was formed, and by the summer of 1888 the vein had been explored by means of a 200-foot vertical shaft and a 750-foot adit. By the summer of 1893, 1,000 tons of silver ore, which had a net value of $25,000, had been mined. The ore was concentrated at Washington Reduction Company's mill at Ruby City. Following the silver panic of 1893, the mine remained inactive until 1905, at which time Arlington Mining Company reopened the mine and undertook development work. Between 1914 and 1921, several thousand tons of ore, which contained 66.6 ounces of silver per ton, was mined at a net profit of $31,000. The mine remained idle until 1937, when Arlington Mines Inc. was formed. The company erected a 50-ton-per-day flotation mill near the portal of the mine's main adit and resumed mining operations. In 1938 and 1939, a total of 5,700 tons of ore that had a net value of $71,683 was concentrated in the mill. Mining and milling operations at the Arlington ceased early in 1940, and in 1945 the company was dissolved.

The Arlington vein is a quartz fissure vein that strikes north and dips 70° west. It is 1 to 6 feet thick and has wall rocks of granodiorite and gneiss. For the most part, the vein occurs along the contact between the granodiorite and gneiss. The ore minerals, which occur as bands in the quartz vein, consist of argentiferous tetrahedrite and galena, chalcopyrite, and minor sphalerite. Parts of the vein that were mined contained ore shoots that were 2 feet thick and as much as 300 feet long. Transverse faults offset parts of the vein as much as 10 feet, while faults, which parallel the vein, have drawn the ore minerals out into thin dark gray bands.

The silver content of that part of the vein that was mined ranged from 10 ounces to as much as 1,000 ounces per ton. However, the average silver content, based on past production, was around 60 ounces. Other metals in the vein occur only in minor amounts; the gold content of ore that was shipped was only 0.02 ounce, and copper was only 1.15 percent. The silver content of the vein that remains in the mine is unknown to the writer. Huntting (1956, p. 300) reports that the 100-foot level of the winze in the main adit contains two ore shoots that total 350 feet in length and average 2.5 feet in thickness. The silver content of the ore shoots averages 18 ounces per ton.

Underground workings in the form of shafts, drifts, and crosscuts have a total length of around 4,500 feet (fig. 4). The workings expose the vein on four levels for a total vertical distance of 540 feet. The main haulage adit is 1,290 feet long and intersects the vein 972 feet from the portal of the adit and 440 feet beneath the outcrop of the vein. From the point where the adit intersects the vein, overhead stopes extend 400 feet north and 200 feet south. Where the adit intersects the vein, a winze has been sunk 100 feet. At 50 and 100 feet below the collar of the winze, two working levels have been developed. The upper adit, which is 200 feet above the main adit, intersects the vein 420 feet from the portal of the adit, and 200 feet beneath the outcrop of the vein. The adit contains over 700 feet of drifts, and a shaft that extends to the surface. The shaft contains several working levels from which ore has been mined.

It is possible that the richest ore shoots in the Arlington vein were removed during past mining operations; however, parts of the vein have yet to be explored. Most likely, future mining operations will be concentrated on that part of the vein that lies beneath the main haulage adit.

Fourth of July

The Fourth of July mine is 1 mile north of the summit of Ruby Hill and in the center of the NW$\frac{1}{4}$ sec. 5, T. 34 N., R. 25 E. A steep unimproved road that ascends the northwestern slope of Ruby Hill provides access to the mine, which is at an elevation of 4,500 feet (fig. 3).

The Fourth of July vein was discovered in April 1887 by R. Dilderback. In 1889, high-grade silver ore was shipped to a smelter at Helena, Montana; this was one of the first shipments of ore to be made from the Ruby mining district. A 200-foot shaft was sunk on the vein, and, on the average, 10 tons of high-grade ore was shipped monthly to smelters. So favorable were the shipments that, in 1890, a Montana syndicate took over the mine and sank a double-compartment shaft to a depth of 500 feet. Silver ore was shipped to the concentrating mill at Ruby City until mid-1893, at which time the mine was forced to shut down because of the silver panic that was sweeping the nation. The total production at this time amounted to $36,000. The mine remained idle until 1958, when Cecil Murray of Okanogan reopened the 200-foot shaft. From 1958 through 1964, Murray shipped hand-sorted ore to the Trail smelter in Canada. Except for a small shipment by C. W. Harkness in 1967, the shipments made by Murray were the last to be made from the district. In the summer and fall of 1972, the mine was being rehabilitated by Ray Jones of Vancouver, Washington.

The Fourth of July vein, which averages 6 feet in thickness, strikes N. 10° W. and dips 70° to 80° E. The vein is in biotite gneiss and parallels a granodiorite-gneiss contact that is several hundred feet west. The metallic minerals of the vein are argentiferous tetrahedrite and galena that are almost always accompanied by pyrite. The minerals appear to be concentrated into a 2-foot-thick section of the vein that parallels the hanging wall. Parts of the vein are highly sheared by faults that parallel the walls of the vein. Early mining operations were confined to ore shoots that contained 50 to 150 ounces of silver

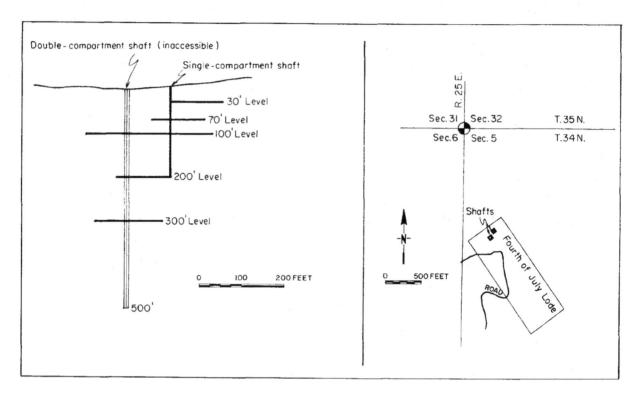

FIGURE 5.—Fourth of July mine workings.

per ton. Ore that was mined in 1964 contained 50 to 80 ounces.

The underground workings at the Fourth of July mine consist of a double-compartment 500-foot shaft and a single-compartment 200-foot shaft that contain several working levels. Drifts extend north and south along the vein at the 100-, 200-, and 300-foot levels of the 500-foot shaft, and south along the vein at the 30-, 70-, and 100-foot levels of the 200-foot shaft (fig. 5). Each level in the 200-foot shaft contains stopes from which ore has been removed. The extent of mining in the 500-foot shaft cannot be determined because the shaft is inaccessible.

Sonny Boy

The Sonny Boy mine is about three-fourths of a mile south of the Arlington and is in the southern part of the SE$\frac{1}{4}$ sec. 31, T. 35 N., R. 25 E., at an elevation of 3,680 feet (fig. 3). The mine workings are 0.2 of a mile east of the Ruby Hill road, but are not visible from the road.

The Sonny Boy vein was discovered in 1886 by George Melvin, who staked it as the Arizona lode claim. Rich parts of the vein contained as much as $260 per ton in gold and silver; however, the average metal content of the vein turned out to be low. Other than several short adits and shafts, very little work was undertaken at the property. In 1935, the property was taken over by Ruby Mountain Mining Company, and, in 1937, 5 tons of ore was shipped to the Tacoma smelter. The returns from this shipment had

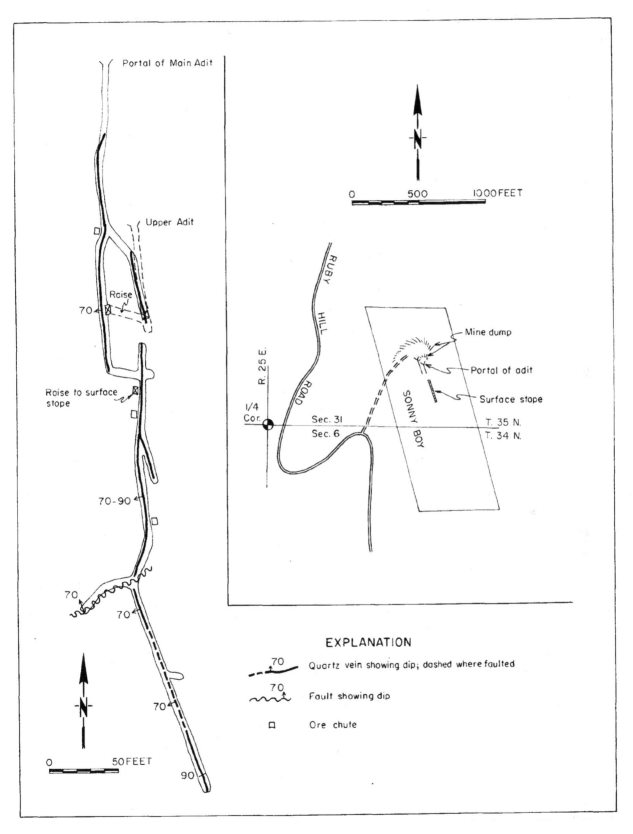

FIGURE 6.—Sonny Boy mine workings.

a net value of $28.64 per ton, which barely paid the mining and transportation costs. Inasmuch as it proved impractical to ship crude ore, a 25-ton flotation mill was built on the property in 1939, and 10 truckloads of lead and copper concentrates were hauled to smelters in Tacoma and Kellogg, Idaho. However, the mining and milling operations were not profitable and mining ceased in 1940.

At the Sonny Boy mine, tetradedrite, galena, chalcopyrite, and sphalerite are sparsely disseminated in two quartz veins. The veins, which range in thickness from 6 inches to 6 feet, strike north and dip steeply west. The host rock for the veins is granodiorite.

The main adit follows the Sonny Boy veins for 600 feet in a southerly direction (fig. 6). The vein has been mined from several small stopes in the adit, as well as from a surface stope. The surface stope extends for 60 feet along the strike of the vein, and up to 30 feet along the dip of the vein. A near-vertical shaft connects the north end of the stope to the main adit and acted as an ore chute during mining operations. The vein in the surface stope is 3 to 4 feet thick, strikes N. 12° W., and dips 75° W. The ore minerals appear to have been concentrated along the footwall part of the vein, inasmuch as only that part of the vein was removed from the stope.

First Thought

The First Thought mine is on the northwest end of Ruby Hill and near the center of the NE¼ sec. 31, T. 35 N., R. 25 E.

Elevations range from 3,000 feet at the mine's main adit, to 3,250 feet at the upper adit. From the old townsite of Ruby City, a steep single-track road may be followed 2½ miles to the main adit (fig. 3).

The First Thought vein was discovered in October 1886 by J. Kladisky, R. Dilderback, and P. McGell, and was one of the first discoveries to be made on Ruby Hill. Soon after its discovery, it was sold to an Oregon syndicate that organized the First Thought Silver Mining Company. A 1½-mile aerial tramline was built from the mine to the concentrating mill at Ruby City; from October 1892 through May 1893, the mine produced silver ore valued at $66,000. Like other mines in the district, mining operations at the First Thought came to an end during the silver panic of 1893. Several small shipments of silver ore were made from the mine in the 1920's, but the production was insignificant. Currently, the mine is idle; and because of caved mine workings, most underground workings are inaccessible.

At the First Thought mine, galena, tetrahedrite, sphalerite, and pyrite occur in discontinuous lenticular masses of quartz that are up to 90 feet thick, and as much as 600 to 700 feet in maximum breadth. The lenses, which have a general strike of N. 10° E. and dip 55° to 60° E., occur in highly foliated feldspathic, quartzitic, and micaeous gneisses. The strikes of the lenses parallel the foliation of the gneisses. The ore minerals are concentrated into ore shoots along the walls of the lenses; some shoots are as much as 5 feet thick. Whereas the ore shoots contain up to 75 to 100 ounces per ton in silver, the massive quartz between ore shoots contains only 6 to 8 ounces.

Underground mine workings at the First Thought mine are in excess of 4,000 feet and are on three levels that have a vertical extent of 350 feet. Adit No. 1, which is the main adit of the mine, is at an elevation of 2,960 feet, and is about 50 feet west of the Ruby Hill road (fig. 7). The adit heads S. 60° E. and is caved at its portal. Judging from the size of the dump, mine workings in the adit probably total 2,000 linear feet. Adit No. 2, the dump of which is barely visible because of trees, is 450 feet south-east of Adit No. 1, and about 150 feet above it. The adit heads S. 75° E. for 65 feet, at which point it becomes inaccessible because of caved ground. At 60 feet from the portal, a drift heads south for an unde-termined distance in caved ground. The dump at the portal of Adit No. 2 suggests at least 700 feet of mine workings. The uppermost adit is 225 feet southeast and 100 feet above Adit No. 2. The adit is caved at its portal, but the size of the dump suggests at least 800 feet of workings. The dumps of the three adits contain abundant vein quartz, which for the most part is barren of ore minerals. However, grains of galena, tetrahedrite, chalcopyrite, and sphalerite are visible in some quartz frag-ments.

Last Chance

The Last Chance mine is near the center of sec. 31, T. 35 N., R. 25 E., at an elevation of 3,000 feet (fig. 3).

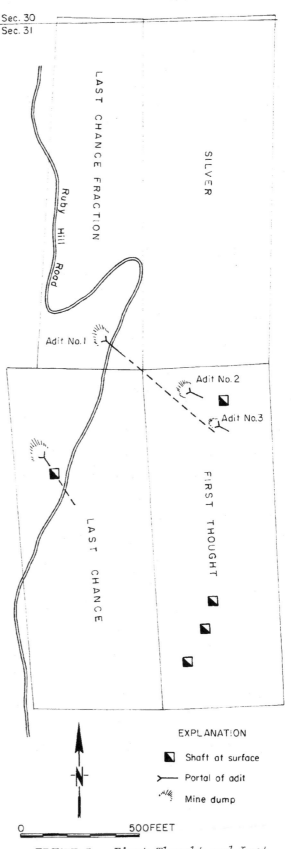

FIGURE 7.—First Thought and Last Chance claim map.

The main mine workings are 0.2 of a mile south of First Thought mine Adit No. 1, and about 1 mile north of the Arlington mine. The mine dump is 100 feet west of, and visible from, the Ruby Hill road (fig. 7).

The Last Chance vein was discovered in October 1886, by John Cluman and James Milliken, and staked as the Ruby lode claim. The claim was sold to Jonathan Bourne, Jr., who patented it in 1904 as the Last Chance Lode. A shaft was sunk to a depth of 300 feet, and, at the 100- and 200-foot levels, drifts were driven along the vein. At the bottom of the shaft, a crosscut was driven 800 feet eastward to intersect the adjoining First Thought vein. Near the collar of the shaft, a 650-foot adit was driven in a southeasterly direction, and ore containing silver, lead, and copper was blocked out. However, because of the collapse of the silver market, the ore was never mined. In 1920, a lessee reopened the mine and shipped ore to a smelter at Bradley, Idaho. The ore averaged 30 ounces of silver, 17 percent lead, and 4 percent copper per ton. Small shipments of ore were made again in 1921 and 1924. Since 1924 the mine has been idle, except for limited exploration work in 1949.

The Last Chance vein is a quartz fissure vein that strikes S. 50° E., and dips 70° SW. It averages 12 feet in thickness and occurs in granodiorite and hornblende-mica schist. In parts of the vein that were mined, argentiferous galena and tetrahedrite, chalcopyrite, and sphalerite were concentrated into ore shoots that were 2 to 4 feet thick and as much as 200 feet long. Between ore shoots, ore

minerals are only sparsely disseminated in the quartz. Parts of the vein have been displaced 6 to 10 feet by transverse faults; the northwest segments of the vein are generally displaced towards the southwest.

The extent of the underground workings at the Last Chance mine are unknown to the writer. Water fills the shaft nearly to its collar, and the adit is caved near its portal.

Nevada (War Eagle, Peacock)

The Nevada mine is on the southeast slope of Peacock Mountain and in the SW$\frac{1}{4}$ NE$\frac{1}{4}$ sec. 30, T. 36 N., R. 25 E., where the elevation is 3,100 feet (fig. 3). From the old townsite of Ruby City, a steep unimproved single-tract road can be followed west for 2 miles to the mine. Currently the mine is being rehabilitated by Silver Consolidated Mining Company of Spokane.

The Nevada vein was discovered in September 1886 by Fred Wendt and others. The vein appeared to be rich in silver and lead, and the War Eagle Mining and Milling Company was organized to explore and develop the deposit. In 1901, the company shipped a carload of ore to a smelter, for which they received only $10 per ton. Inasmuch as crude ore could not be shipped at a profit, mining operations ceased. In 1915, Peacock Mining and Milling Company took over the mine, as well as 32 mining claims on Peacock Mountain, and undertook an extensive exploration and development program. From the west bank of Salmon Creek, about one-half mile north of Ruby City, a crosscut was started that would,

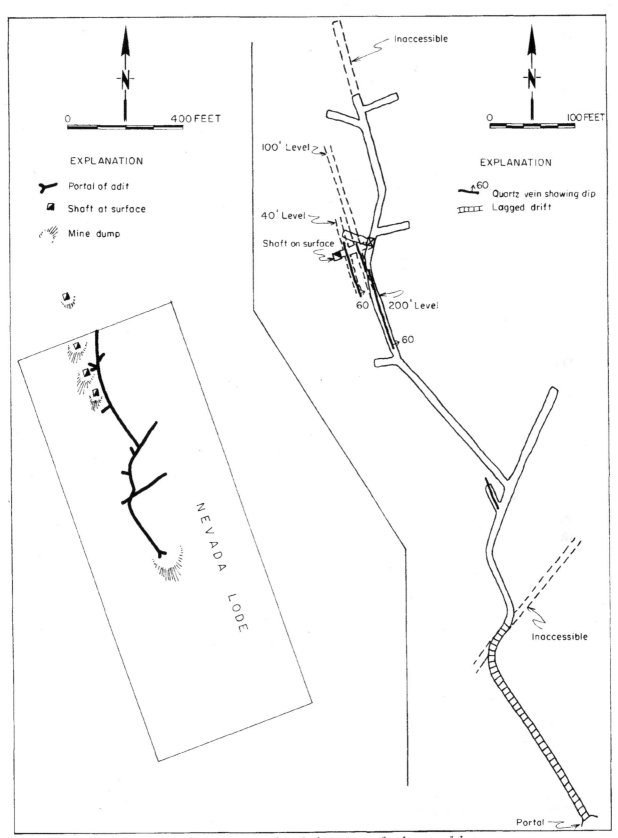

FIGURE 8.—Nevada claim map and mine workings.

at 2,100 feet from its portal, intersect the veins on Peacock Mountain at depths of up to 1,500 feet beneath the surface. After the crosscut was driven 750 feet, the project was abandoned and work at the property ceased. In 1923 and 1924, lessees made several small shipments of lead and copper ore to smelters; however, returns from the shipments did not exceed mining costs, and once again mining operations at the Nevada mine ceased. In 1954, Conconully Mines, Inc. undertook mining at the property and shipped ore through 1957. This operation was somewhat successful, inasmuch as the ore was concentrated at a flotation mill at Omak prior to being shipped to smelters.

The Nevada vein is the most persistant of several metallized quartz veins on Peacock Mountain. It is in hornblende-biotite schist and quartz diorite gneiss, and parallels the foliation of gneiss and schist. The vein has a general strike of N. 15° W., dips 60° E., and is 3 to 5 feet thick. Ore minerals consist of galena, tetrahedrite, chalcopyrite, and sphalerite that are almost always accompanied by pyrite. The ore minerals are sparsely disseminated in the veins, or they are concentrated into bands up to 1 foot thick that parallel the walls of the vein. The silver occurs mainly in the galena and tetrahedrite but is appreciably lower than the silver-bearing veins of Ruby Hill. Tetrahedrite occurs near the surface, but at 100 feet beneath the surface chalcopyrite is the predominant copper mineral. The average silver content of ore shoots is only around 4.5 ounces. Ore that was shipped in 1956 contained 5.75 ounces of silver per ton. Representative samples from an ore shoot on the 40-foot level of the mine contained 3.0 to 4.3 ounces. In addition to silver, the ore contained 3.6 to 8.6 percent lead, 3.15 percent zinc, and 0.2 to 0.7 percent copper.

Underground mine workings at the Nevada mine consist of four shafts, the deepest of which is 220 feet, several hundred feet of drifts, and a 1,000-foot adit (fig. 8). Most mining has taken place in the 220-foot shaft. The vein has been drifted upon at the 40- and 100-foot levels, and the bottom of the shaft intersects the main adit. Faults offset the vein at several places in the drifts and adits. North of the shaft, on the 40- and 100-foot levels, a steeply-dipping fault offsets the north segment of the vein, about 35 feet to the west. In the adit, 25 feet south of the shaft, the vein is cut off by another fault. When the writer examined the property in 1972, none of the workings were accessible. All shafts were caved at their collars, and the main adit was caved at its portal. The dumps of two shafts that are 150 feet and 250 feet north of the 220-foot shaft indicate that each shaft is about 100 feet deep.

Wheeler (Mineral Hill)

The Wheeler mine is on the southeast slope of Mineral Hill at an elevation of 3,275 feet. It is in the center of sec. 2, T. 35 N., R. 24 E., and 1½ miles west of Conconully (fig. 3). Two miles of dirt road provide access from Conconully to the main adit of the mine.

The Columbia claim, which is one of several patented mining claims in the vicinity

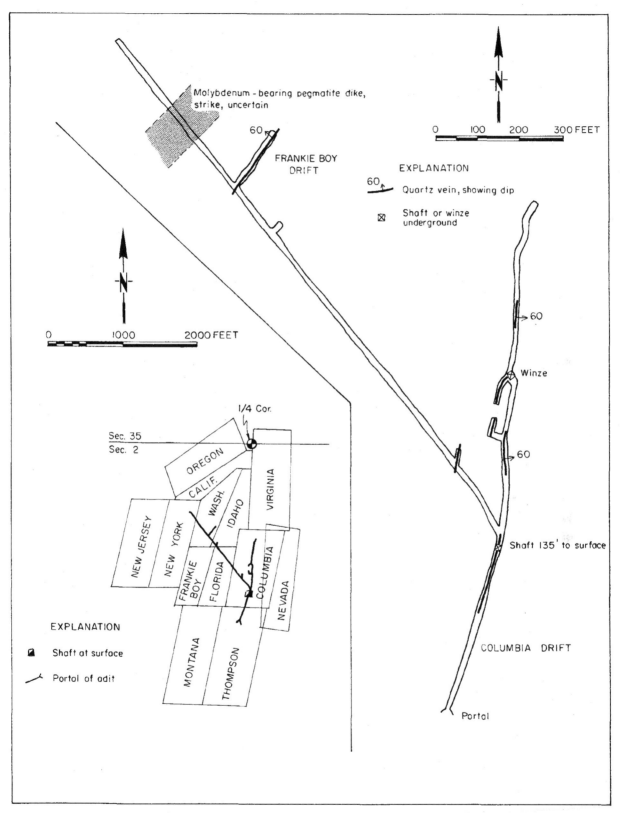

FIGURE 9.—Wheeler mine claim map and mine workings.

of the Wheeler mine, was staked in 1886 by William Daniels and E. P. Wheeler. It, along with several other claims, was acquired by Bridgeport Mining & Milling Company who had the claims patented in 1896. A shaft was sunk on the Columbia vein, and small shipments of high-grade silver ore were made; however, much of the ore proved to be of milling grade and could not be shipped to distant smelters at a profit. In 1902, Mineral Hill Mining Company was formed to develop the mineral deposits on Mineral Hill. An adit was started on the Columbia vein, and by 1906 the vein had been drifted upon for about 1,000 feet. In the Columbia adit a crosscut was driven in a northwesterly direction an additional 1,000 feet for the purpose of exploring other veins that cropped out on Mineral Hill. In 1937, a 20-ton flotation mill was built near the portal of the Columbia adit, and during 1938 and 1939 small amounts of lead-silver concentrates were produced. Since 1940, several companies have undertaken limited development work at the Wheeler mine. Much of the work was done by Sunny Peak Mining Company.

The Columbia vein is the main vein at the Wheeler mine. It is a quartz fissure vein in granodiorite and contains disseminated grains of galena, chalcopyrite, sphalerite, tetraherite, and pyrite. In parts of the vein, the ore minerals are concentrated into ore shoots up to 1 foot wide that parallel the walls of the vein. The vein strikes N. 10° E., dips 60° E., and is 6 inches to 3 feet thick. The wallrock adjacent to the vein has been hydrothermally altered and subjected to post-metallization shearing.

The silver occurs mainly in argentiferous galena and tetrahedrite; minor stephanite has been reported, but the writer was unable to confirm its presence. Parts of the vein that have a high lead content are proportionally high in silver. According to Aughey (1907, p. 3a), the vein averages 34 ounces per ton in silver, and 10 percent lead. The average gold content is 0.22 ounce per ton, and copper is negligible.

Underground workings at the Wheeler mine consist of almost 3,000 feet of drifts, crosscuts, and shafts (fig. 9). The main adit follows the Columbia vein for 1,200 feet. About 420 feet from the portal, a shaft has been driven 135 feet to the surface. Around 700 feet from the portal, a winze has been sunk to an undetermined depth on the vein. At 466 feet from the portal, a crosscut extends 1,440 feet to the northwest. Many quartz veins, which are from 1 to 20 inches thick, are intersected by the crosscut; however, most veins are only sparsely metallized with galena, chalcopyrite, and pyrite. The Frankie Boy vein is the richest vein in the crosscut and consists of 1 foot of white granular quartz. The vein strikes N. 35° E., dips 60° NW., and contains scattered grains and small lenses of galena, tetrahedrite, chalcopyrite, and pyrite. The granodiorite wall rock contains abundant sericite. The vein has been drifted upon for 165 feet, mainly in a northeasterly direction, and parts of the vein contain up to several hundred dollars per ton in silver, lead, and gold.

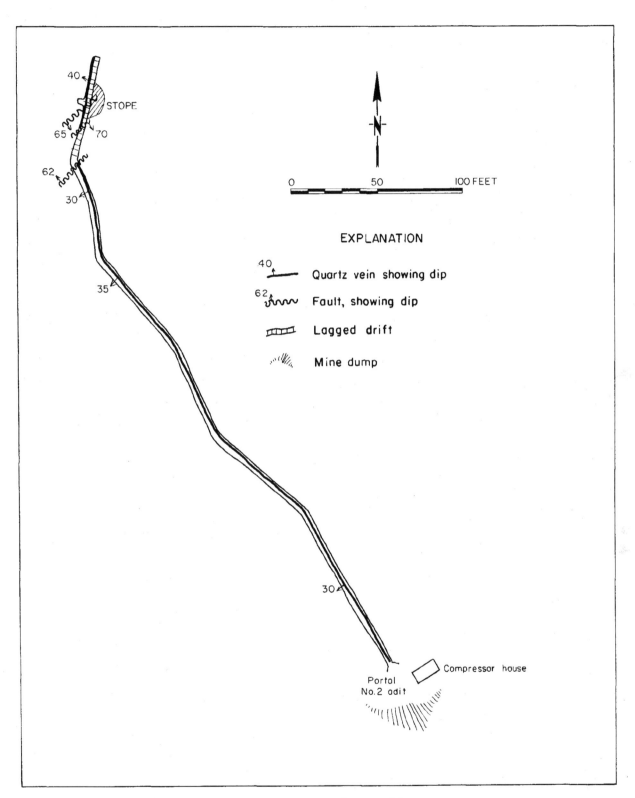

FIGURE 10.—Mohawk mine workings.

About 140 feet beyond the Frankie Boy vein, the crosscut encounters a north-striking molybdenite-bearing pegmatite dike that is 100 feet thick. Jones (1916, p. 21) describes the dike as follows:

> The dike differs in character from place to place. Quartz in places is the chief mineral, in other places cellular quartz contains much sericite in fine druses, and in still others the rock is coarse granite in which the feldspars are unaltered. The molybdenite occurs in this rock in thin flakes and radial nodules about a quarter of an inch in diameter. It is more abundant in association with quartz and sericite, but was also noted in the less altered granite or pegmatite. Its occurrence in the pegmatite is sporadic and nowhere is it abundant enough to mine.

The crosscut continues for 350 feet beyond the molybdenite-bearing dike, but does not expose any valuable veins.

Mohawk

The Mohawk mine is on the southeastern slope of Mineral Hill and in the $S\frac{1}{2}SW\frac{1}{4}SE\frac{1}{4}$ sec. 31, T. 36 N., R. 24 E. (fig. 3). A dirt road from Conconully provides access to the main adit that is at an elevation of about 4,000 feet.

The mine was worked as early as 1890 by Henry Lawrence, who drove two short adits on a quartz vein that contained up to 65 ounces per ton in silver. However, like other mines in the district, work at the Mohawk ceased during the silver panic of 1893. In 1951, the mine was reopened by Sunny Peak Mining Company, and ore, which contained as much as 60 ounces of silver, was produced until 1954. In 1961

and 1967, small shipments of silver ore were made to the Trail smelter by lessees. The mine has been idle since 1967; however, in 1972, Silver Consolidated Mining Company was rehabilitating the mine.

The Mohawk vein, as exposed for 500 feet in the No. 2 Adit, consists of $1\frac{1}{2}$ to 3 feet of quartz that fills a fissure in porphyritic granodiorite (fig. 10). The vein has a general strike of N. 30° W., and dips 30° to 40° SW. In the last 50 feet of the adit, the vein is sheared and faulted, and strikes N. 10° E., and dips 45° W. Parts of the vein, especially in the last 50 feet of the adit, contain coarse-grained galena, chalcopyrite, and pyrite, and fine-grained tetrahedrite. Some of the ore minerals are concentrated into bands up to 1 foot wide that contain as much as 60 ounces per ton of silver, 13 percent lead, and 3 percent copper.

In Adit No. 1, which is 350 feet north of, and 225 feet higher than Adit No. 2, the Mohawk vein has been drifted upon for around 150 feet. The adit is not accessible because of a caved portal. Ore that is stockpiled near the portal of the adit contains around 10 percent galena, 10 percent chalcopyrite, and minor sphalerite and tetrahedrite.

Lone Star

The Lone Star mine is on the west bank of Salmon Creek, 1 mile north of Conconully (fig. 3). It is near the $E\frac{1}{4}$ cor. sec. 36, T. 36 N., R. 24 E., at an elevation of around 2,480 feet. From Conconully, a good county road leads to within several hundred feet of the mine.

The Lone Star vein was discovered in the spring of 1886 by Henry C. Lawrence, and was one of the first discoveries to be made in the Conconully district. By 1890, an incline shaft had been sunk on the vein to a depth of around 350 feet, and ore that contained up to 200 ounces per ton in silver and 30 percent lead was mined from several

levels. By 1897, around $40,000 had been spent developing the mine, but production amounted to only several thousand dollars. In the years that followed, several attempts were made to place the mine back into production, but all attempts failed. Trial shipments of ore were made to smelters in 1913, 1943, and 1969. Favorable returns from the 1969 shipment encouraged Silver Consolidated Mining Company of Spokane to undertake construction of a flotation mill at the

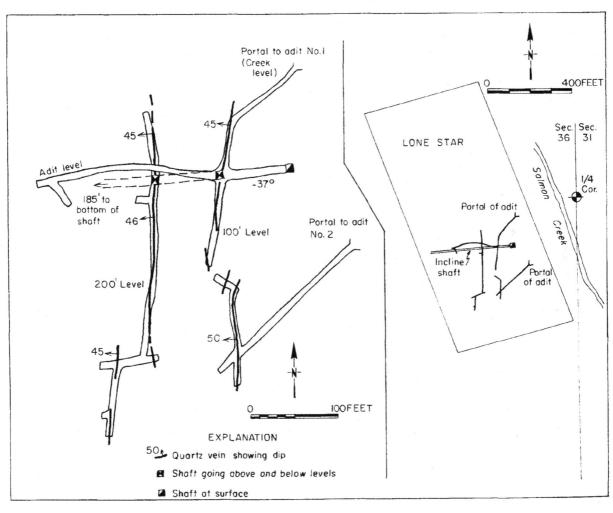

FIGURE 11.—Lone Star claim map and mine workings.

mine; however, the mill was never completed.

At the Lone Star mine, galena, sphalerite, chalcopyrite, tetrahedrite, and pyrite occur in quartz fissure veins in sheared and sericitized granodiorite. The main vein, which has an average thickness of 3 feet, strikes north, and dips 45° to 50° W. On the south end of the vein, where shearing and faulting in the granodiorite is prominent, the vein consists of as much as 12 feet of banded quartz. The south end of the vein has been offset as much as 50 feet by faults. The ore minerals for the most part are only sparsely scattered throughout the vein. In some parts of the vein, the ore minerals are concentrated into bands up to several feet wide that parallel the walls of the vein. Assays of up to 20 ounces per ton in silver, 5.5 percent lead, and 2.2 percent zinc have been obtained from the bands.

The Lone Star mine contains over 2,000 feet of underground workings in the form of shafts, drifts, and crosscuts (fig. 11). The main shaft, which is on a minus 37° incline and heads S. 85° W., has working levels at 100, 200, and 300 feet. On the 100-foot level, the vein has been drifted upon for 110 feet north and 60 feet south. This level also reaches the surface 110 feet north and 67 feet south of the shaft's collar. On the 200-foot level, a drift follows the vein 75 feet north and 205 feet south. The extent of the workings on the 300-foot level are unknown to the writer. About 110 feet southeast of, and 15 feet lower than the collar of the shaft, an adit has been driven southwest 170 feet. Near the face of the adit, a sparsely metallized quartz vein, which contains galena, sphalerite, chalcopyrite, and pyrite, has been drifted upon 35 feet south and 105 feet north. It does not appear that ore was ever mined in this adit.

MISCELLANEOUS MINES AND PROSPECTS

The mines and prospects in the list that follows were obtained from data on file at Washington State Division of Mines and Geology, and from references listed at the end of this report. Other mining properties are present in the Conconully area, but little is known about them.

The list of the mines and prospects is broken down into three separate areas, which are as follows: (1) Ruby Hill-Peacock Mountain area, (2) Mineral Hill area, (3) Conconully-Salmon Creek area. The number that follows the property name is the number assigned to that property on the property location map (fig. 3).

Ruby Hill-
Peacock Mountain Area

Woo Loo Moo Loo Prospect (1)

Location: $NE\frac{1}{4}NE\frac{1}{4}$ sec. 32, T. 34 N., R. 25 E.; elevation 3,000 ft.

Geology: 8-foot-thick quartz vein in biotite-hornblende gneiss.

Ore minerals: Galena and tetrahedrite.

Development: 150-foot shaft.

Production: None.

References: Huntting, 1956, p. 305; Bethune, 1891, p. 52-53.

Keystone Prospect (2)

Location: S½NW¼ sec. 5, T. 34 N., R. 25 E.; elevation 4,600 ft.

Geology: 8-foot-thick quartz vein in biotite gneiss. Vein strikes N. 10° W., and dips 25° E. Contains up to 50 ounces of silver.

Ore minerals: Tetrahedrite and galena.

Development: 150-foot shaft.

Production: None.

References: Huntting, 1956, p. 305; Bethune, 1891, p. 52-53.

Hughes Prospect (5)

Location: Center W½ sec. 6, T. 34 N., R. 25 E.; elevation 2,960 ft.

Geology: Sparsely metallized shear zones and quartz veins in granodiorite.

Ore minerals: Chalcopyrite, galena, sphalerite, and molybdenite.

Development: 100- and 40-foot adits.

Production: None.

Reference: Ralph Miller, owner of property.

Plant-Callahan Mine (9)

Location: NE¼NE¼ sec. 32, T. 35 N., R. 25 E.; elevation 2,600 ft.

Geology: Quartz veins in biotite gneiss. Veins average less than 1 foot thick, strike northwest, and dip steeply northeast.

Ore minerals: Galena and tetrahedrite.

Development: 175- and 65-foot adits.

Production: $6,000 prior to 1900.

References: Huntting, 1956, p. 308; Jones, 1916, p. 31.

Johnny Boy Prospect (12)

Location: Center sec. 24, T. 35 N., R. 24 E.; elevation 4,000 ft.

Geology: 10-inch-thick quartz vein in granodiorite. Vein strikes N. 20° E., and dips 50° SE.

Ore minerals: Galena, chalcopyrite, and sphalerite.

Development: 30-foot incline shaft.

Production: Unknown.

References: Mines and Geology field notes.

Mineral Hill Area

Leuena Mine (15)

Location: SE¼SW¼ sec. 35, T. 36 N., R. 24 E.; elevation 4,400 ft.

Geology: 7-foot-thick quartz vein in granodiorite. Vein strikes N. 55° E. and is vertical. High-grade ore contained 200 to 800 ounces of silver.

Development: 50- and 75-foot shafts; 60-foot adit, and 70-foot crosscut.

Production: Several carloads prior to 1890.

Ore minerals: Tetradedrite, stephanite, and argentite.

References: Huntting, 1956, p. 305; Bethune, 1891, p. 59; Jones, 1916, p. 28-29.

Conconully-Salmon Creek Area

Gubser Prospect (16)

Location: S½SW¼SW¼ sec. 31, T. 36 N., R. 25 E.; elevation 2,400 ft.

Geology: Quartz veins 1 to 2 feet thick in granodiorite. Veins strike N. 5° E., and dip 85° NW.

Gubser Prospect (16) - Continued

Ore minerals: Galena, sphalerite, and scheelite.

Development: 900-foot adit, with 170 feet of drifts.

Production: None.

References: Huntting, 1956, p. 219; Culver and Broughton, 1945, p. 44.

John Arthur Prospect (18)

Location: SE$\frac{1}{4}$NE$\frac{1}{4}$ sec. 36, T. 36 N., R. 24 E.; elevation 2,550 ft.

Geology: Quartz vein in granodiorite. Vein 10 feet thick, with 2-foot pay-streak that contains up to 100 ounces per ton of silver. Vein strikes N. 45° E., and dips 60° W.

Ore minerals: Argentite and native silver.

Development: 70-foot incline shaft.

Production: None.

References: Huntting, 1956, p. 305; Bethune, 1892, p. 98.

Tough Nut Mine (19)

Location: Center NW$\frac{1}{4}$ sec. 31, T. 36 N., R. 25 E.; elevation 3,200 ft.

Geology: Quartz vein in quartz-mica schist. Vein 3 to 10 feet wide, strikes N. 25° W., and dips 60° SW. Ore mined contained 47 to 86 ounces silver and 32 to 43 percent lead.

Ore minerals: Galena, sphalerite, and chalcopyrite.

Development: 50-foot incline shaft, and 250-foot adit, with 40-foot winze.

Production: $9,000 prior to 1901.

References: Huntting, 1956, p. 311; Bethune, 1891, p. 55-56; Jones, 1916, p. 25; Gage, 1941, p. 209.

Homestake Mine (20)

Location: E$\frac{1}{2}$SW$\frac{1}{4}$ sec. 31, T. 36 N., R. 25 E.; elevation 3,200 ft.

Geology: 11-foot thick quartz vein in quartz-mica schist. Vein strikes N. 22° W., and dips 30° SW. Ore mined contained 18 to 56 ounces of silver and 32 to 36 percent lead.

Ore minerals: Galena.

Development: 29-foot shaft, and 175-foot adit, with 42 foot crosscut.

Production: 400 tons prior to 1902, of which 100 tons netted $1,500.

References: Huntting, 1956, p. 220; Bethune, 1891, p. 56.

Key Mine (21)

Location: SW$\frac{1}{4}$NW$\frac{1}{4}$ sec. 31, T. 36 N., R. 25 E.; elevation 2,800 ft.

Geology: Sparsely metallized quartz vein in mica schist and migmatite. Vein 3 to 10 feet thick, strikes N. 25° E., and dips 60° NW.

Ore minerals: Galena, sphalerite, and chalcopyrite.

Development: 300-foot adit, 80-foot shaft, and 105-foot drift.

Production: 1,500 tons; 12 tons in 1914 netted $444 in silver and lead.

References: Huntting, 1956, p. 304; Jones, 1916, p. 25; Gage, 1941, p. 207.

Monitor Mine (22)

Location: NW$\frac{1}{4}$NW$\frac{1}{4}$ sec. 31, T. 36 N., R. 25 E.; elevation 2,800 ft.

Geology: 2-foot-thick quartz vein in mica schist. Vein strikes N. 20° E., dips 70° NW., and contains up to 35 ounces of silver and 10 percent lead.

Ore minerals: Galena, sphalerite, and chalcopyrite.

Development: 200-foot adit, and 50-foot shaft.

Monitor Mine (22) – Continued

Production: Shipment in 1889 netted $250 per ton in silver.

References: Huntting, 1956, p. 221; Bethune, 1892, p. 107; Jones, 1916, p. 27.

Salmon River Prospect (23)

Location: $E\frac{1}{2}NE\frac{1}{4}SW\frac{1}{4}$ sec. 31, T. 36 N., R. 25 E.; elevation 3,200 ft.

Geology: Four quartz veins from 1 to 5 feet thick in mica schist. Veins strike N. 35° W., and dip 30° to 60° SW. Parts of some veins contained up to 4 ounces in gold, 83 ounces in silver, and 20 percent lead.

Ore minerals: Galena, argentite, tetrahedrite, sphalerite, and chalcopyrite.

Development: 150–foot crosscut with 500 feet of drifts, 20– and 30–foot adits, and 20–foot crosscut.

Production: Unknown.

References: Huntting, 1956, p. 309; Jones, 1916, p. 26; Bethune, 1891, p. 56–58.

Copper King Prospect (24)

Location: Center sec. 31, T. 36 N., R. 25 E.; elevation 3,400 ft.

Geology: Quartz vein in mica schist. Vein 7 feet thick, strikes N. 40° W., and dips 55° SW.

Ore minerals: Galena, sphalerite, and chalcopyrite.

Development: 100– and 50–foot adits.

Production: None.

References: Huntting, 1956, p. 218; Jones, 1916, p. 26.

Esther Prospect (25)

Location: $SW\frac{1}{4}NE\frac{1}{4}$ sec. 31, T. 36 N., R. 25 E.; elevation 3,500 ft.

Geology: Sparsely metallized quartz vein in mica schist. Vein 1 to 3 feet thick, strikes north, and dips 70° W.

Ore minerals: Galena, sphalerite, and chalcopyrite.

Development: 100– and 50-foot adits.

Production: None.

References: Huntting, 1956, p. 218; Jones, 1916, p. 26.

Lady of the Lake Prospect (26)

Location: Center $NE\frac{1}{4}$ sec. 6, T. 35 N., R. 25 E.; elevation 2,400 ft.

Geology: Sparsely metallized quartz vein in mica schist. Vein 3 to 5 feet thick, strikes N. 15° E., and dips 45° W. Vein on surface contained up to 120 ounces of silver.

Ore minerals: Galena, sphalerite, chalcopyrite, scheelite, and molybdenite.

Development: 130-foot adit, with 30 feet of drifts.

References: Huntting, 1956, p. 305; Jones, 1916, p. 29; Bethune, 1891, p. 29; Culver and Broughton, 1945, p. 43.

Silver King Mine (27)

Location: Center $SW\frac{1}{4}$ sec. 31, T. 36 N., R. 25 E.; elevation 2,500 ft.

Geology: Quartz vein in granodiorite. Vein several inches to 3 feet wide, strikes N. 15° E., and dips 60° NW.

Ore minerals: Galena, sphalerite, chalcopyrite, tetraherite, scheelite, and molybdenite.

Development: 240-foot adit, 100-foot incline shaft, and 130-foot drift.

Production: Minor lead and silver.

References: Huntting, 1956, p. 223; Culver and Broughton, 1945, p. 43.

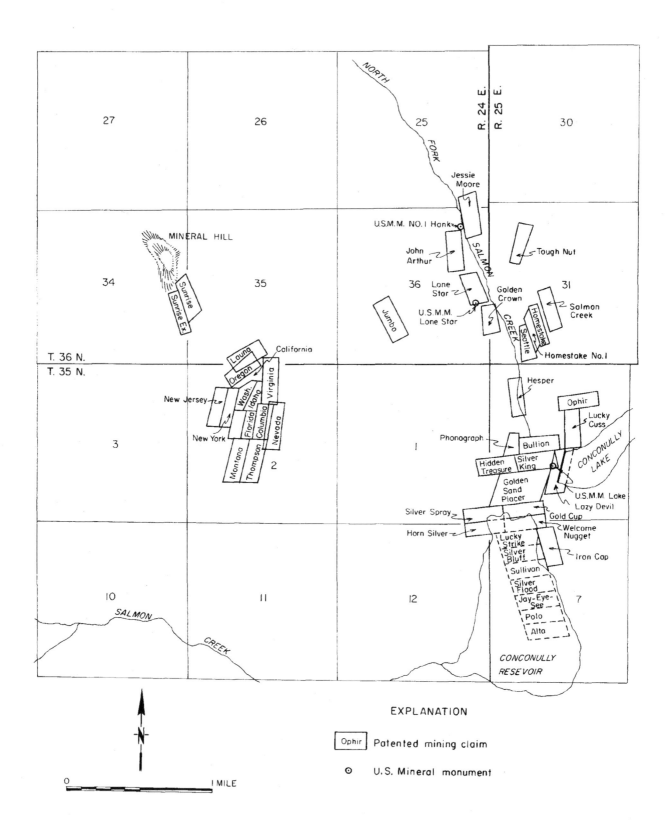

FIGURE 12.—Patented mining claims of the Conconully area.

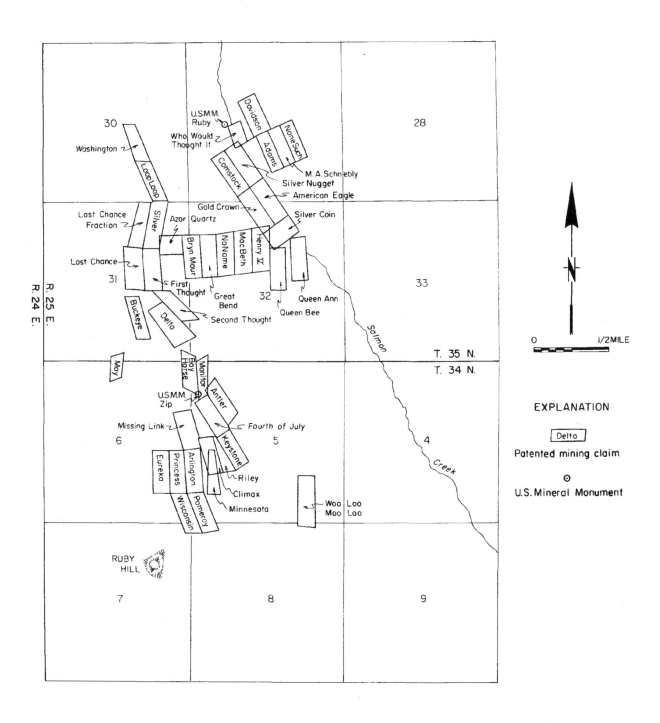

FIGURE 13.—Patented mining claims of the Ruby Hill area.

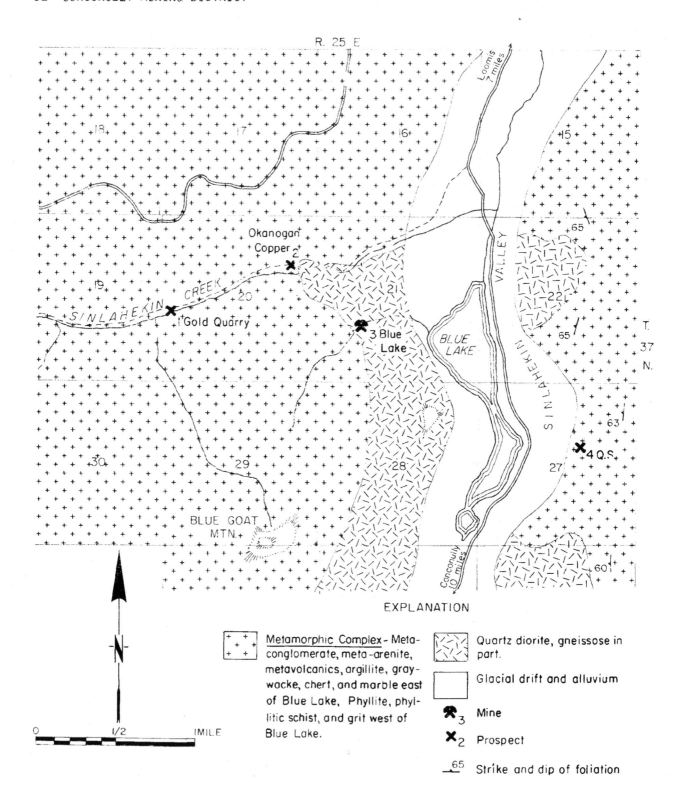

EXPLANATION

Metamorphic Complex - Meta-conglomerate, meta-arenite, metavolcanics, argillite, graywacke, chert, and marble east of Blue Lake. Phyllite, phyllitic schist, and grit west of Blue Lake.

Quartz diorite, gneissose in part.

Glacial drift and alluvium

Mine

Prospect

Strike and dip of foliation

FIGURE 14.—General geology and mines and prospects of the Blue Lake area.

BLUE LAKE AREA

Three prospects and one mine are in the vicinity of Blue Lake, which is 10 miles north of Conconully (fig. 14). The properties contain minor copper and gold that lead to exploration work in the early 1900's; however, ore was produced at only one mine. In 1901, Blue Lake mine produced 5,000 tons of copper-gold ore of unknown value. Since 1901, only limited exploration work has been undertaken at the mineral deposits near Blue Lake.

Sinlahekin Valley, in which Blue Lake lies, contains thick deposits of glacial drift and alluvium. East of Blue Lake, the predominant rocks are pre-Jurassic metaconglomerate, meta-arenite, meta-andesite, marble, and chert that are intruded by late Mesozoic quartz diorite. West of the lake, the quartz diorite intrudes pre-Jurassic phyllite and phyllitic schist.

Metallization in the Blue Lake area consists of sparsely scattered grains of chalcopyrite that occur in pyritized quartz veins and pyritized metamorphic rocks. At the Q. S. prospect, chalcopyrite occurs in pyritized argillite and pyritized metavolcanics. At the Gold Quarry and Okanogan Copper prospects, chalcopyrite is sparsely disseminated in beds of pyritized argillite. At the Blue Lake mine, quartz fissure veins in quartz diorite contain sparsely disseminated grains of chalcopyrite. Although parts of some deposits contain up to 3 percent copper, the average copper content is probably less than 1 percent. Gold and silver occur only in trace amounts in the pyritized rocks; however, rocks that contain chalcopyrite are somewhat richer in gold and silver.

The principal mines and prospects of the Blue Lake area are as follows:

Gold Quarry Prospect

Location: $W\frac{1}{4}$ cor. sec. 20, T. 37 N., R. 25 E.; elevation 2,400 ft.

Geology: Sparsely pyritized beds of argillite in phyllitic schist.

Ore minerals: Chalcopyrite.

Development: Open cuts, short adits, and shallow shafts.

Production: None.

Reference: Jones, 1916, p. 36; Huntting, 1956, p. 140.

Okanogan Copper Prospect

Location: $E\frac{1}{2}NE\frac{1}{4}$ sec. 20, T. 37 N., R. 25 E.; elevation 2,160 ft.

Geology: Pyritized shale near quartz diorite-shale contact.

Ore minerals: Chalcopyrite.

Development: 500-foot adit at creek level; short adits at 2,260 and 3,000 feet elevation, northwest of the main adit.

Production: None.

References: Jones, 1916, p. 35; Huntting, 1956, p. 145.

Blue Lake Mine

Location: Center $SW\frac{1}{4}$ sec. 21, T. 37 N., R. 25 E.; elevation 3,100 ft.

Geology: Quartz veins, 1 to 3 feet thick in quartz diorite.

Ore minerals: Chalcopyrite.

Development: 300-foot adit.

Production: 5,000 tons in 1901.

Blue Lake Mine - Continued

References: Jones, 1916, p. 35; Landes, 1902, p. 33; Huntting, 1956, p. 63.

G. S. Prospect

Location: Center sec. 27, T. 37 N., R. 25 E.; elevation 2,000 to 4,000 ft.

Geology: Pyritized argillite and metavolcanics.

Ore minerals: Chalcopyrite.

Development: 1,060- and 600-foot adits, and several shallow shafts.

Production: None.

References: Jones, 1916, p. 34; Landes, 1902, p. 32; Huntting, 1956, p. 69.

GALENA AREA

The Galena area is 6 miles east of Conconully and 2 miles south of Mud Lake. Most of the prospects and mines of this area fall within sec. 31, T. 36 N., R. 26 E. Prior to the organization of the Conconully mining district in 1900, the Galena area fell within the Galena mining district that was organized in 1886.

Little has been written on the prospects and mines of the Galena area, and only one mine has a record of production. Silver Bluff mine, which was operated by Montana & Washington Mining & Milling Company from 1922 through 1926, produced copper-silver ore valued at $80,000.

The veins of the Galena area are quartz fissure veins in Triassic limestone and quartzite. They are 2 to 4 feet thick and contain up to

100 ounces in silver per ton, as well as up to 3.9 percent copper. The silver minerals of the veins are reported to be argentite and stromeyerite. Copper minerals include azurite, malachite, and chalcocite. For the most part the ore minerals are confined to pockets in the quartz veins.

The principal properties of the Galena area, as reported by Huntting (1956), are as follows:

Silver Bluff Mine

Location: NE$\frac{1}{4}$ sec. 31, T. 36 N., R. 26 E.

Deposit: Quartz vein, 2 feet wide on surface. Assays 97 to 110 ounces in silver, and 2.9 to 3.5 percent copper.

Ore minerals: Chalcocite and argentite.

Development: 65-foot incline shaft.

Production: $80,000 to end of 1923.

Silver Bell Prospect

Location: NE$\frac{1}{4}$ sec. 31, T. 36 N., R. 26 E.

Deposit: Quartz vein, 2$\frac{1}{2}$ feet wide.

Ore minerals: Chalcocite, argentite, and stromeyerite.

Eureka Prospect

Location: NE$\frac{1}{4}$ sec. 31, T. 36 N., R. 26 E.

Deposit: Quartz vein, 4 feet wide. Assays up to 0.01 ounce gold, 370 ounces silver, and 3.9 percent copper.

Ore minerals: Chalcocite and argentite.

Lulu Prospect

Location: NE$\frac{1}{4}$ sec. 31, T. 36 N., R. 26 E.

Lulu Prospect - Continued

Deposit: Quartz vein, 4 feet wide. Assays up to 0.01 ounce gold, 320 ounces silver, and 0.04 percent copper.

Ore minerals: Chalcocite and argentite.

Black Huzzar Prospect

Location: NE$\frac{1}{4}$ sec. 31, T. 36 N., R. 26 E.

Deposit: Quartz vein, 3$\frac{1}{2}$ feet wide. Assays up to 90 ounces silver and 3.5 percent copper.

Ore minerals: Chalcocite and argentite.

Belcher Prospect

Location: E$\frac{1}{2}$SE$\frac{1}{4}$ sec. 25, T. 36 N., R. 25 E.

Deposit: Unknown.

Development: 275-foot shaft with drifts at the 100- and 275-foot levels.

ISOLATED OCCURRENCES

Carl Frederick (Bernhardt)

The Carl Frederick prospect, which is also known as the Bernhardt mine, is on the west slope of Clark Peak, 1$\frac{1}{2}$ miles south of Tiffany Mountain. The main adit of the prospect is about 500 feet west of the E$\frac{1}{4}$ cor. sec. 3, T. 36 N., R. 23 E. and at an elevation of 7,040 feet. From the Boulder Creek road near Roger Lake, a trail leads 1$\frac{1}{2}$ miles east to the prospect, the adits of which are plainly visible on a grassy slope above timberline.

The Carl Frederick vein is a quartz fissure vein that strikes N. 30° E., and dips 35° to 40° NW. It is 4 to 24 inches thick and is in medium-grained granodiorite. The vein contains scattered grains of galena and pyrite; in some parts of the vein, galena is concentrated into ore shoots that are up to 1 foot thick.

According to Patty (1921, p. 257), the vein has been drifted upon for 400 feet. Galena is scanty in the first 350 feet of the adit, but in the last 50 feet it is more abundant. Near the face of the adit, a winze has been sunk 38 feet on the galena-rich vein. Twenty feet below the collar of the winze the vein has been drifted upon for short distances, and 200 to 300 tons of ore, which averages 20 ounces of silver per ton, is present in the drifts.

About 250 feet west of, and 150 feet below the main adit, another adit was driven northeasterly 270 feet in an attempt to intersect the downward extension of the galena-rich vein that is exposed in the main adit. The vein was not encountered in this lower adit because the adit passes beneath the northwesterly-dipping vein. However, the vein should be encountered at about 150 feet, should a crosscut be driven northwest from the face of the adit.

When the writer examined the property in 1970, the lower adit was accessible, but the main adit was caved near its portal.

Starr

The Starr mine is 5 airline miles west of Tonasket and near the headwaters of Aeneas Creek. The mine's main adit is near the

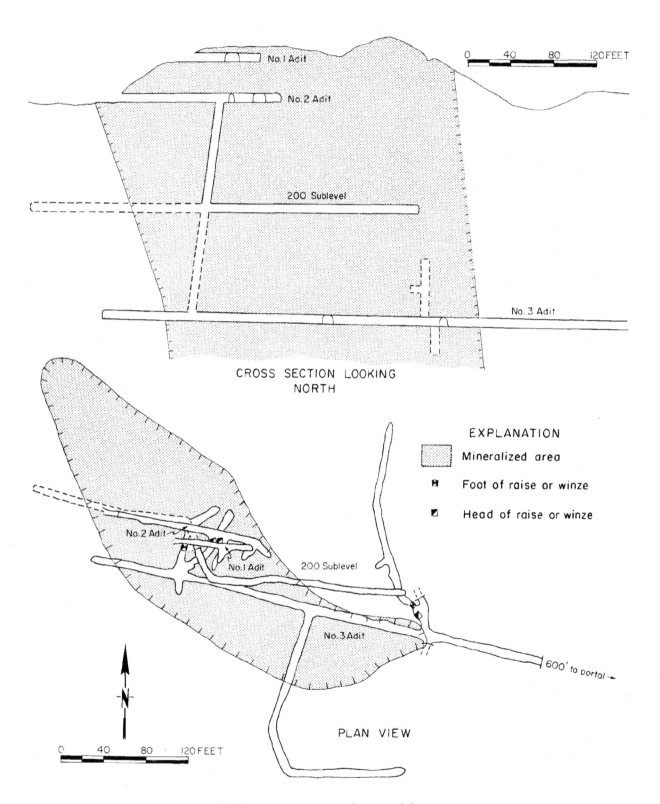

CROSS SECTION LOOKING
NORTH

EXPLANATION

Mineralized area

Foot of raise or winze

Head of raise or winze

PLAN VIEW

FIGURE 15.—Starr mine workings.

center of the SE$\frac{1}{4}$ sec. 8, T. 37 N., R. 26 E. and at an elevation of 3,200 feet. The mine is presently owned by Wilbur Hallauer of Oroville. A detailed description of the Starr mine may be found in "Molybdenum Occurrences of Washington" (Purdy, 1954, p. 51-62).

The Starr molybdenum occurrence was discovered by Andrew Starr in 1915. In 1928, Molybdenum Corporation of America explored the deposit, but found that the rock was not sufficiently metallized to justify a mining operation. A total of 2,600 feet of drifts, crosscuts, and raises was driven by the company. From 1935 through 1947, Titanium Alloy Manufacturing Company of New York held an option on the property. They drove several hundred feet of raises and winzes and dug several surface pits and one shaft. Up until 1939, no ore had been shipped from the mine, but, in 1939, Carl Lundstrom shipped about 3,000 tons of ore to his mill at Nighthawk, Washington. In 1967, the mine was leased by Cambri Mining and Development Ltd. of Canada. The company undertook geochemical and geophysical surveys on the property and diamond drilled the deposit; however, the mine never reached the production stage. In 1970, the deposit was core drilled by Bear Creek Mining Company, and, in 1971 and 1972, Natural Resources Development Corporation undertook geochemical and geophysical surveys.

At the Starr mine, molybdenite and pyrite occur as disseminations and fracture coatings in silicified granodiorite and in quartz veins. The outline of the metallized zone is in the shape of an elongated ellipse that is 300 to 400 feet long and 50 to 130 feet wide (fig. 15). The depth to which the metallized zone extends is in excess of several hundred feet. Silicification varies in intensity throughout the deposit, and because of many irregular, intersecting fractures, the deposit is blocky. Oxidation extends to a depth of around 100 feet, and the molybdenite in the open fractures of the oxidized zone has to a great extent been removed. Possibly as much as 50 percent of the molybdenite content in the near-surface part of the oxidized zone is in the form of molybdite, a hydrous ferric molybdate.

The total length of the underground mine workings at the Starr mine is around 3,000 feet. The workings consist of three adits, one sublevel, and several raises, winzes, and crosscuts (fig. 15). It is estimated that the deposit contains in excess of 1 million tons of indicated and inferred ore that averages around 0.30 percent of equivalent MoS_2.

Central (Trinidad)

This mine is 8.5 miles southwest of Tonasket and on the south shore of Turtle Lake, which is in the NE$\frac{1}{4}$ sec. 9, T. 36 N., R. 26 E.

In the vicinity of Turtle Lake, brecciated and silicified black argillite has been intruded by an aplite porphyry dike. The dike, which appears to be several hundred feet wide, trends north. Parts of the dike contain pods of galena and pyrite that is accompanied by minor sphalerite and chalcopyrite. A shaft has been sunk 50 feet on the dike, and, at 32 and 50 feet below the collar of the shaft, short drifts have been driven. Galena-bearing rock from the shaft contains 6 to 8 ounces of silver per ton. From the 32-foot level of the shaft, Trinidad Mining & Smelting Company, in 1918, shipped 30 tons of ore that averaged $12 per ton in silver and gold.

Short adits and shafts occur elsewhere on the property; however, they appear to have been driven mainly in pyritized porphyry and argillite.

Tonasket (Montgomery)

This prospect is 6 miles south of Tonasket and 1 mile west of the Okanogan River. It is near the NE. cor. sec. 12, T. 36 N., R. 26 E.

The predominant rock in the vicinity of the prospect is schistose calcareous argillite that contains disseminated pyrite. A limy bed in the argillite is reported to contain fluorite (Huntting, 1956, p. 71). Huntting also reports the presence of chalcopyrite, molybdenite, huebnerite, tungstite, and galena in gangue consisting of quartz and fluorite. At one place, huebnerite constitutes 5 percent of a vein.

Metallization at the Tonasket prospect has been explored by a 200-foot adit and several open cuts.

Sherman

The Sherman mine is 3 miles northwest of Omak in sec. 20, T. 34 N., R. 26 E. A good county road provides access to the mine, the workings of which are at elevations of 1,400 to 1,800 feet.

The original discoveries at the Sherman mine were made by Ezra Sherman in 1916. In the years that followed, Mr. Sherman explored his discoveries of lead, zinc, copper, gold, and silver by driving adits and sinking shafts on the largest metallized veins. In order to more extensively explore the deposits, the Sherman Mining Company was organized by W. W. and C. C. Sherman in 1945. Core drilling was undertaken, and in the late 1950's a double-compartment shaft was sunk to a depth of 220 feet. In 1958, around 500 tons of lead-zinc-silver ore was mined. The ore was concentrated at a flotation mill near Omak prior to being shipped to the smelter. In 1972, core drilling was once again underway at the mine.

Ore minerals at the Sherman mine occur in several shear zones near a granite-rhyolite contact that trends northwest, and dips 30° to 45° SW. The shear zones, which are 2 to 11 feet thick, strike northwest to northeast, and have westerly dips of 20° to 90°. On the Standard claim, a 4-foot-thick metallized shear zone, consisting of gouge, talc, sericite, and silicified breccia, occurs along the granite-rhyolite contact. A 100-foot incline shaft has been sunk on the contact and exposes gouge and breccia that contain pyrite, arsenopyrite, galena, and sphalerite. The sulfides appear to be concentrated into a 1-foot-thick zone that is adjacent to the granite footwall of the shear zone. Rock from the shear zone assayed 0.03 ounce gold, 10 ounces silver, 1.7 percent lead, and 0.67 percent zinc.

On the Brook claim, a 40-foot incline shaft has been sunk on a 2-foot-wide vertical

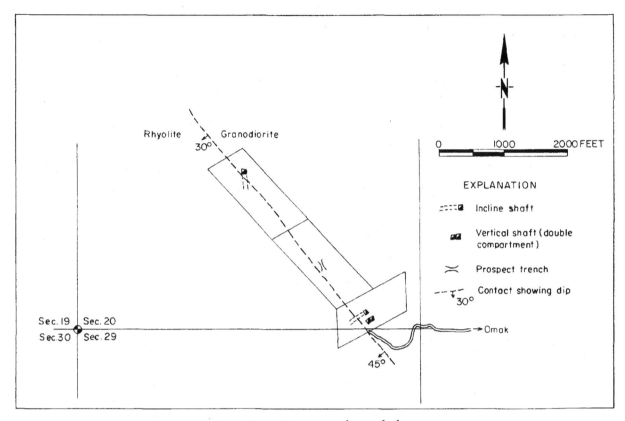

FIGURE 16.—Sherman mine claim map.

shear zone that strikes N. 57° E. in coarse-grained granite. Breccia from the shaft contains scattered grains of pyrite, arseno-pyrite, galena, and sphalerite. Assays of selected dump samples show 0.08 ounce gold, 31 ounces silver, 3.5 percent lead, and 2.15 percent zinc.

About 200 feet southeast of the incline shaft on the Brook claim, a vertical double-compartment shaft has been sunk in granite for 220 feet. The shaft contains over 400 feet of drifts and crosscuts that explore four metallized shear zones. The shear zones, which are $4\frac{1}{2}$ to 11 feet thick, strike N. 40° to 45° W., and dip 60° to 70° SW. The Sherman Mining Company reports that the shear zones contain 4 to 7.7 percent lead, 5.8 to 8.1 percent zinc, and 3.9 to 7 ounces of silver per ton. Copper and gold occur only in minor amounts.

Buck Mountain (Buckhorn)

This prospect is 2 miles south of the summit of Buck Mountain and is in the $NW\frac{1}{4}$ $NE\frac{1}{4}$ sec. 33, T. 34 N., R. 24 E. From the Loup Loup Highway, the Sweat Creek road may be followed to within several hundred feet of the prospect.

The Buck Mountain vein is a quartz fissure vein in medium-grained biotite granodiorite. The vein contains sparsely scattered grains of tetrahedrite, fine-grained scheelite, and pyrite. Some scheelite also occurs as thin veinlets in the quartz.

In the lower adit, which is about 100 feet long, the vein is only 2 to 6 inches thick, strikes N. 45° W., and dips 60° SW. In the upper adit, which is also about 100 feet long, the vein is 2 to 3 feet thick, strikes N. 30° to 40° W., and dips 70° SW. About 60 feet from the portal, a winze has been sunk to an unknown depth on the vein. The vein is also exposed in several trenches and shallow prospect pits, which together with the underground workings, suggest a length of at least 500 feet for the vein.

Huntting (1956, p. 344) reports that one shipment of silver ore was made from the property. However, the time, amount, and value of the shipment remains unknown.

OUTLOOK FOR THE DISTRICT

Several mines in the Conconully area are sufficiently metallized to become producing mines. Current (1973) metal prices (silver, $2.20 oz.; lead, 15 cents lb.) make the ores valuable mainly for silver and lead. Large-scale production cannot be expected from most mines; however, several properties should be able to produce small amounts of ore that contains up to 50 ounces of silver per ton and up to 10 percent lead.

The mines on Mineral Hill are fairly accessible. Those on Ruby Hill present problems, mainly because of flooded shafts and caved workings. Currently, plans are underway to reopen the Mohawk mine on Mineral Hill, the Nevada mine on Peacock Mountain, and the Fourth of July mine on Ruby Hill.

Much of the ore in the Conconully area is of milling grade, but this should present no problems. Jones (1916, p. 24) reports that concentration of plus 40 minus 100 mesh size material on a Wilfley table removed 80 percent of the sulfides at a concentration ratio of $4\frac{1}{2}$ to 1. Material finer than 100 mesh, when subjected to flotation, yielded 73 percent of the sulfides at a concentration ratio of $3\frac{1}{2}$ to 1. The concentrates would have to be shipped to a lead or copper smelter for the extraction of the silver from the argentiferous tetrahedrite and galena.

Although current molybdenum prices ($1.72/lb., MoS_2) do not appear favorable for mining operations at the Starr molybdenum mine, an increase in the price of molybdenum could result in renewed mining.

SELECTED REFERENCES

Aughey, Samuel, 1907, Report on mining claims on Mineral Hill in Okanogan County, Washington: Washington Div. Mines and Geology open-file report.

Bethune, G. A., 1891, Mines and minerals of Washington: Washington State Geologist, 1st Annual Report, 122 p.

Bethune, G. A., 1892, Mines and minerals of Washington: Washington State Geologist, 2nd Annual Report, 183 p.

Culver, H. E.; Broughton, W. A., 1945, Tungsten resources of Washington: Washington Div. Geology Bull. 34, 89 p.

Gage, H. L., 1941, The lead-zinc mines of Washington: U.S. Bonneville Power Administration, Market Development Section, 235 p.

Goldsmith, Richard, 1952, Petrology of the Tiffany-Conconully area, Okanogan County, Washington: Univ. of Washington Ph. D. thesis, 356 p.

Griffith, R. F., 1949, Economic geology of Peacock Mountain, Okanogan County, Washington: Univ. of Washington M.S. thesis, 63 p.

Hodges, L. K., 1897, Mining in the Pacific Northwest: The Seattle Post-Intelligencer, Seattle, Wash., 183 p.

Huntting, M. T., 1956, Inventory of Washington minerals, Part 2 — Metallic minerals: Washington Div. Mines and Geology Bull. 37, pt. 2, 428 p.

Jones, E. L., Jr., 1916, Reconnaissance of the Conconully and Ruby mining districts, Washington: U.S. Geol. Survey Bull. 640-B, p. 11-36.

Landes, Henry; and others, 1902, The metalliferous resources of Washington, except iron: Washington Geol. Survey Annual Report 1901, pt. 2, 123 p.

Menzer, F. J., 1964, Geology of the crystalline rocks west of Okanogan, Washington: Univ. of Washington Ph. D. thesis, 64 p.

Patty, E. N., 1921, The metal mines of Washington: Washington Geol. Survey Bull. 23, 366 p.

Purdy, C. P., Jr., 1954, Molybdenum occurrences of Washington: Washington Div. Mines and Geology Rept. Inv. 18, 118 p.

U.S. Bureau of Mines, 1932-1965, Minerals Yearbook.

U.S. Geological Survey, 1904-1931, Mineral Resources of the United States.

Washington Division of Mines and Geology, Field notes and mining property files.

Western Historical Publishing Company, 1904, An illustrated history of Stevens, Ferry, Okanogan, and Chelan Counties, State of Washington: Western Historical Publishing Company, Spokane, 867 p.

www.GoldMiningBooks.com

Books On Mining

Visit: www.goldminingbooks.com to order your copies or ask your favorite book seller to offer them.

Mining Books by Kerby Jackson

Gold Dust: Stories From Oregon's Mining Years - Oregon mining historian and prospector, Kerby Jackson, brings you a treasure trove of seventeen stories on Southern Oregon's rich history of gold prospecting, the prospectors and their discoveries, and the breathtaking areas they settled in and made homes. 5" X 8", 98 ppgs. Retail Price: $11.99

The Golden Trail: More Stories From Oregon's Mining Years - In his follow-up to "Gold Dust: Stories of Oregon's Mining Years", this time around, Jackson brings us twelve tales from Oregon's Gold Rush, including the story about the first gold strike on Canyon Creek in Grant County, about the old timers who found gold by the pail full at the Victor Mine near Galice, how Iradel Bray discovered a rich ledge of gold on the Coquille River during the height of the Rogue River War, a tale of two elderly miners on the hunt for a lost mine in the Cascade Mountains, details about the discovery of the famous Armstrong Nugget and others. 5" X 8", 70 ppgs. Retail Price: $10.99

Oregon Mining Books

Geology and Mineral Resources of Josephine County, Oregon - Unavailable since the 1970's, this important publication was originally compiled by the Oregon Department of Geology and Mineral Industries and includes important details on the economic geology and mineral resources of this important mining area in South Western Oregon. Included are notes on the history, geology and development of important mines, as well as insights into the mining of gold, copper, nickel, limestone, chromium and other minerals found in large quantities in Josephine County, Oregon. 8.5" X 11", 54 ppgs. Retail Price: $9.99

Mines and Prospects of the Mount Reuben Mining District - Unavailable since 1947, this important publication was originally compiled by geologist Elton Youngberg of the Oregon Department of Geology and Mineral Industries and includes detailed descriptions, histories and the geology of the Mount Reuben Mining District in Josephine County, Oregon. Included are notes on the history, geology, development and assay statistics, as well as underground maps of all the major mines and prospects in the vicinity of this much neglected mining district. 8.5" X 11", 48 ppgs. Retail Price: $9.99

The Granite Mining District - Notes on the history, geology and development of important mines in the well known Granite Mining District which is located in Grant County, Oregon. Some of the mines discussed include the Ajax, Blue Ribbon, Buffalo, Continental, Cougar-Independence, Magnolia, New York, Standard and the Tillicum. Also included are many rare maps pertaining to the mines in the area. 8.5" X 11", 48 ppgs. Retail Price: $9.99

Ore Deposits of the Takilma and Waldo Mining Districts of Josephine County, Oregon - The Waldo and Takilma mining districts are most notable for the fact that the earliest large scale mining of placer gold and copper in Oregon took place in these two areas. Included are details about some of the earliest large gold mines in the state such as the Llano de Oro, High Gravel, Cameron, Platerica, Deep Gravel and others, as well as copper mines such as the famous Queen of Bronze mine, the Waldo, Lily and Cowboy mines. This volume also includes six maps and 20 original illustrations. 8.5" X 11", 74 ppgs. Retail Price: $9.99

Metal Mines of Douglas, Coos and Curry Counties, Oregon - Oregon mining historian Kerby Jackson introduces us to a classic work on Oregon's mining history in this important re-issue of Bulletin 14C Volume 1, otherwise known as the Douglas, Coos & Curry Counties, Oregon Metal Mines Handbook. Unavailable since 1940, this important publication was originally compiled by the Oregon Department of Geology and Mineral Industries includes detailed descriptions, histories and the geology of over 250 metallic mineral mines and prospects in this rugged area of South West Oregon. 8.5" X 11", 158 ppgs. Retail Price: $19.99

Metal Mines of Jackson County, Oregon - Unavailable since 1943, this important publication was originally compiled by the Oregon Department of Geology and Mineral Industries includes detailed descriptions, histories and the geology of over 450 metallic mineral mines and prospects in Jackson County, Oregon. Included are such famous gold mining areas as Gold Hill, Jacksonville, Sterling and the Upper Applegate. 8.5" X 11", 220 ppgs. Retail Price: $24.99

Metal Mines of Josephine County, Oregon - Oregon mining historian Kerby Jackson introduces us to a classic work on Oregon's mining history in this important re-issue of Bulletin 14C, otherwise known as the Josephine County, Oregon Metal Mines Handbook. Unavailable since 1952, this important publication was originally compiled by the Oregon Department of Geology and Mineral Industries includes detailed descriptions, histories and the geology of over 500 metallic mineral mines and prospects in Josephine County, Oregon. 8.5" X 11", 250 ppgs. Retail Price: $24.99

Metal Mines of North East Oregon - Oregon mining historian Kerby Jackson introduces us to a classic work on Oregon's mining history in this important re-issue of Bulletin 14A and 14B, otherwise known as the North East Oregon Metal Mines Handbook. Unavailable since 1941, this important publication was originally compiled by the Oregon Department of Geology and Mineral Industries and includes detailed descriptions, histories and the geology of over 750 metallic mineral mines and prospects in North Eastern Oregon. 8.5" X 11", 310 ppgs. Retail Price: $29.99

Metal Mines of North West Oregon - Oregon mining historian Kerby Jackson introduces us to a classic work on Oregon's mining history in this important re-issue of Bulletin 14D, otherwise known as the North West Oregon Metal Mines Handbook. Unavailable since 1951, this important publication was originally compiled by the Oregon Department of Geology and Mineral Industries and includes detailed descriptions, histories and the geology of over 250 metallic mineral mines and prospects in North Western Oregon. 8.5" X 11", 182 ppgs. Retail Price: $19.99

Mines and Prospects of Oregon - Mining historian Kerby Jackson introduces us to a classic mining work by The Oregon Bureau of Mines in this important re-issue of The Handbook of Mines and Prospects of Oregon. Unavailable since 1916, this publication includes important insights into hundreds of gold, silver, copper, coal, limestone and other mines that operated in the State of Oregon around the turn of the 19th Century. Included are not only geological details on early mines throughout Oregon, but also insights into their history, production, locations and in some cases, also included are rare maps of their underground workings. 8.5" X 11", 314 ppgs. Retail Price: $24.99

Lode Gold of the Klamath Mountains of Northern California and South West Oregon (See California Mining Books)

Mineral Resources of South West Oregon - Unavailable since 1914, this publication includes important insights into dozens of mines that once operated in South West Oregon, including the famous gold fields of Josephine and Jackson Counties, as well as the Coal Mines of Coos County. Included are not only geological details on early mines throughout South West Oregon, but also insights into their history, production and locations. 8.5" X 11", 154 ppgs. Retail Price: $11.99

Chromite Mining in The Klamath Mountains of California and Oregon (See California Mining Books)

Southern Oregon Mineral Wealth - Unavailable since 1904, this rare publication provides a unique snapshot into the mines that were operating in the area at the time. Included are not only geological details on early mines throughout South West Oregon, but also insights into their history, production and locations. Some of the mining areas include Grave Creek, Greenback, Wolf Creek, Jump Off Joe Creek, Granite Hill, Galice, Mount Reuben, Gold Hill, Galls Creek, Kane Creek, Sardine Creek, Birdseye Creek, Evans Creek, Foots Creek, Jacksonville, Ashland, the Applegate River, Waldo, Kerby and the Illinois River, Althouse and Sucker Creek, as well as insights into local copper mining and other topics. 8.5" X 11", 64 ppgs. Retail Price: $8.99

Geology and Ore Deposits of the Takilma and Waldo Mining Districts - Unavailable since the 1933, this publication was originally compiled by the United States Geological Survey and includes details on gold and copper mining in the Takilma and Waldo Districts of Josephine County, Oregon. The Waldo and Takilma mining districts are most notable for the fact that the earliest large scale mining of placer gold and copper in Oregon took place in these two areas. Included in this report are details about some of the earliest large gold mines in the state such as the Llano de Oro, High Gravel, Cameron, Platerica, Deep Gravel and others, as well as copper mines such as the famous Queen of Bronze mine, the Waldo, Lily and Cowboy mines. In addition to geological examinations, insights are also provided into the production, day to day operations and early histories of these mines, as well as calculations of known mineral reserves in the area. This volume also includes six maps and 20 original illustrations. 8.5" X 11", 74 ppgs. Retail Price: $9.99

Gold Mines of Oregon - Oregon mining historian Kerby Jackson introduces us to a classic work on Oregon's mining history in this important re-issue of Bulletin 61, otherwise known as "Gold and Silver In Oregon". Unavailable since 1968, this important publication was originally compiled by geologists Howard C. Brooks and Len Ramp of the Oregon Department of Geology and Mineral Industries and includes detailed descriptions, histories and the geology of over 450 gold mines Oregon. Included are notes on the history, geology and gold production statistics of all the major mining areas in Oregon including the Klamath Mountains, the Blue Mountains and the North Cascades. While gold is where you find it, as every miner knows, the path to success is to prospect for gold where it was previously found. **8.5" X 11", 344 ppgs. Retail Price: $24.99**

Mines and Mineral Resources of Curry County Oregon - Originally published in 1916, this important publication on Oregon Mining has not been available for nearly a century. Included are rare insights into the history, production and locations of dozens of gold mines in Curry County, Oregon, as well as detailed information on important Oregon mining districts in that area such as those at Agness, Bald Face Creek, Mule Creek, Boulder Creek, China Diggings, Collier Creek, Elk River, Gold Beach, Rock Creek, Sixes River and elsewhere. Particular attention is especially paid to the famous beach gold deposits of this portion of the Oregon Coast. **8.5" X 11", 140 ppgs. Retail Price: $11.99**

Chromite Mining in South West Oregon - Originally published in 1961, this important publication on Oregon Mining has not been available for nearly a century. Included are rare insights into the history, production and locations of nearly 300 chromite mines in South Western Oregon. **8.5" X 11", 184 ppgs. Retail Price: $14.99**

Mineral Resources of Douglas County Oregon - Originally published in 1972, this important publication on Oregon Mining has not been available for nearly forty years. Included are rare insights into the geology, history, production and locations of numerous gold mines and other mining properties in Douglas County, Oregon. **8.5" X 11", 124 ppgs. Retail Price: $11.99**

Mineral Resources of Coos County Oregon - Originally published in 1972, this important publication on Oregon Mining has not been available for nearly forty years. Included are rare insights into the geology, history, production and locations of numerous gold mines and other mining properties in Coos County, Oregon. **8.5" X 11", 100 ppgs. Retail Price: $11.99**

Mineral Resources of Lane County Oregon - Originally published in 1938, this important publication on Oregon Mining has not been available for nearly seventy five years. Included are extremely rare insights into the geology and mines of Lane County, Oregon, in particular in the Bohemia, Blue River, Oakridge, Black Butte and Winberry Mining Districts. **8.5" X 11", 82 ppgs. Retail Price: $9.99**

Mineral Resources of the Upper Chetco River of Oregon: Including the Kalmiopsis Wilderness - Originally published in 1975, this important publication on Oregon Mining has not been available for nearly forty years. Withdrawn under the 1872 Mining Act since 1984, real insight into the minerals resources and mines of the Upper Chetco River has long been unavailable due to the remoteness of the area. Despite this, the decades of battle between property owners and environmental extremists over the last private mining inholding in the area has continued to pique the interest of those interested in mining and other forms of natural resource use. Gold mining began in the area in the 1850's and has a rich history in this geographic area, even if the facts surrounding it are little known. Included are twenty two rare photographs, as well as insights into the Becca and Morning Mine, the Emmly Mine (also known as Emily Camp), the Frazier Mine, the Golden Dream or Higgins Mine, Hustis Mine, Peck Mine and others. **8.5" X 11", 64 ppgs. Retail Price: $8.99**

Gold Dredging in Oregon - Originally published in 1939, this important publication on Oregon Mining has not been available for nearly seventy five years. Included are extremely rare insights into the history and day to day operations of the dragline and bucketline gold dredges that once worked the placer gold fields of South West and North East Oregon in decades gone by. Also included are details into the areas that were worked by gold dredges in Josephine, Jackson, Baker and Grant counties, as well as the economic factors that impacted this mining method. This volume also offers a unique look into the values of river bottom land in relation to both farming and mining, in how farm lands were mined, re-soiled and reclamated after the dredges worked them. Featured are hard to find maps of the gold dredge fields, as well as rare photographs from a bygone era. **8.5" X 11", 86 ppgs. Retail Price: $8.99**

Quick Silver Mining in Oregon - Originally published in 1963, this important publication on Oregon Mining has not been available for over fifty years. This publication includes details into the history and production of Elemental Mercury or Quicksilver in the State of Oregon. **8.5" X 11", 238 ppgs. Retail Price: $15.99**

Mines of the Greenhorn Mining District of Grant County Oregon - Originally published in 1948, this important publication on Oregon Mining has not been available for over sixty five years. In this publication are rare insights into the mines of the famous Greenhorn Mining District of Grant County, Oregon, especially the famous Morning Mine. Also included are details on the Tempest, Tiger, Bi-Metallic, Windsor, Psyche, Big Johnny, Snow Creek, Banzette and Paramount Mines, as well as prospects in the vicinities in the famous mining areas of Mormon Basin, Vinegar Basin and Desolation Creek. Included are hard to find mine maps and dozens of rare photographs from the bygone era of Grant County's rich mining history. **8.5" X 11", 72 ppgs. Retail Price: $9.99**

Geology of the Wallowa Mountains of Oregon: Part I (Volume 1) - Originally published in 1938, this important publication on Oregon Mining has not been available for nearly seventy five years. Included are details on the geology of this unique portion of North Eastern Oregon. This is the first part of a two book series on the area. Accompanying the text are rare photographs and historic maps.**8.5" X 11", 92 ppgs. Retail Price: $9.99**

Geology of the Wallowa Mountains of Oregon: Part II (Volume 2) - Originally published in 1938, this important publication on Oregon Mining has not been available for nearly seventy five years. Included are details on the geology of this unique portion of North Eastern Oregon. This is the first part of a two book series on the area. Accompanying the text are rare photographs and historic maps.**8.5" X 11", 94 ppgs. Retail Price: $9.99**

Field Identification of Minerals For Oregon Prospectors - Originally published in 1940, this important publication on Oregon Mining has not been available for nearly seventy five years. Included in this volume is an easy system for testing and identifying a wide range of minerals that might be found by prospectors, geologists and rockhounds in the State of Oregon, as well as in other locales. Topics include how to put together your own field testing kit and how to conduct rudimentary tests in the field. This volume is written in a clear and concise way to make it useful even for beginners. **8.5" X 11", 158 ppgs. Retail Price: $14.99**

The Bohemia Mining District of Oregon - Originally published in 1900, this important publication on Oregon Mining has not been available for over a century. Included in this volume are important insights into the famous Bohemia Mining District of Oregon, including the histories and locations of important gold mines in the area such as the Ophir Mine, Clarence, Acturas, Peek-a-boo, White Swan, Combination Mine, the Musick Mine, The California, White Ghost, The Mystery, Wall Street, Vesuvius, Story, Lizzie Bullock, Delta, Elsie Dora, Golden Slipper, Broadway, Champion Mine, Knott, Noonday, Helena, White Wings, Riverside and others. Also included are notes on the nearby Blue River Mining District. **8.5" X 11", 58 ppgs. Retail Price: $9.99**

The Gold Fields of Eastern Oregon - Unavailable since 1900, this publication was originally compiled by the Baker City Chamber of Commerce Offering important insights into the gold mining history of Eastern Oregon, "The Gold Fields of Eastern Oregon" sheds a rare light on many of the gold mines that were operating at the turn of the 19th Century in Baker County and Grant County in North Eastern Oregon. Some of the areas featured include the Cable Cove District, Baisely-Elhorn, Granite, Red Boy, Bonanza, Susanville, Sparta, Virtue, Vaughn, Sumpter, Burnt River, Rye Valley and other mining districts. Included is basic information on not only many gold mines that are well known to those interested in Eastern Oregon mining history, but also many mines and prospects which have been mostly lost to the passage of time. Accompanying are numerous rare photos **8.5" X 11", 78 ppgs. Retail Price: $10.99**

Gold Mining in Eastern Oregon - Originally published in 1938, this important publication on Oregon Mining has not been available for over a century. Included in this volume are important insights into the famous mining districts of Eastern Oregon during the late 1930's. Particular attention is given to those gold mines with milling and concentrating facilities in the Greenhorn, Red Boy, Alamo, Bonanza, Granite, Cable Cove, Cracker Creek, Virtue, Keating, Medical Springs, Sanger, Sparta, Chicken Creek, Mormon Basin, Connor Creek, Cornucopia and the Bull Run Mining Districts. Some of the mines featured include the Ben Harrison, North Pole-Columbia, Highland Maxwell, Baisley-Elkhorn, White Swan, Balm Creek, Twin Baby, Gem of Sparta, New Deal, Gleason, Gifford-Johnson, Cornucopia, Record, Bull Run, Orion and others. Of particular interest are the mill flow sheets and descriptions of milling operations of these mines. **8.5" X 11", 68 ppgs. Retail Price: $8.99**

The Gold Belt of the Blue Mountains of Oregon - Originally published in 1901, this important publication on Oregon Mining has not been available for over a century. Included in this volume are rare insights into the gold deposits of the Blue Mountains of North East Oregon, including the history of their early discovery and early production. Extensive details are offered on this important mining area's mineralogy and economic geology, as well as insights into nearby gold placers, silver deposits and copper deposits. Featured are the Elkhorn and Rock Creek mining districts, the Pocahontas district, Auburn and Minersville districts, Sumpter and Cracker Creek, Cable Cove, the Camp Carson district, Granite, Alamo, Greenhorn, Robinsonville, the Upper Burnt River Valley and Bonanza districts, Susanville, Quartzburg, Canyon Creek, Virtue, the Copper Butte district, the North Powder River, Sparta, Eagle Creek, Cornucopia, Pine Creek, Lower Powder River, the Upper Snake River Canyon, Rye Valley, Lower Burnt River Valley, Mormon Basin, the Malheur and Clarks Creek districts, Sutton Creek and others. Of particular interest are important details on numerous gold mines and prospects in these mining districts, including their locations, histories, geology and other important information, as well as information on silver, copper and fire opal deposits. **8.5" X 11", 250 ppgs. Retail Price: $24.99**

Mining in the Cascades Range of Oregon - Originally published in 1938, this important publication on Oregon Mining has not been available for over seventy five years. Included in this volume are rare insights into the gold mines and other types of metal mines in the Cascades Mountain Range of Oregon. Some of the important mining areas covered include the famous Bohemia Mining District, the North Santiam Mining District, Quartzville Mining District, Blue River Mining District, Fall Creek Mining District, Oakridge District, Zinc District, Buzzard-Al Sarena District, Grand Cove, Climax District and Barron Mining District. Of particular interest are important details on over 100 mines and prospects in these mining districts, including their locations, histories, geology and other important information. **8.5" X 11", 170 ppgs. Retail Price: $14.99**

Beach Gold Placers of the Oregon Coast - Originally published in 1934, this important publication on Oregon Mining has not been available for over 80 years. Included in this volume are rare insights into the beach gold deposits of the State of Oregon, including their locations, occurance, composition and geology. Of particular interest is information on placer platinum in Oregon's rich beach deposits. Also included are the locations and other information on some famous Oregon beach mines, including the Pioneer, Eagle, Chickamin, Iowa and beach placer mines north of the mouth of the Rogue River. **8.5" X 11", 60 ppgs. Retail Price: $8.99**

Idaho Mining Books

Gold in Idaho - Unavailable since the 1940's, this publication was originally compiled by the Idaho Bureau of Mines and includes details on gold mining in Idaho. Included is not only raw data on gold production in Idaho, but also valuable insight into where gold may be found in Idaho, as well as practical information on the gold bearing rocks and other geological features that will assist those looking for placer and lode gold in the State of Idaho. This volume also includes thirteen gold maps that greatly enhance the practical usability of the information contained in this small book detailing where to find gold in Idaho. **8.5" X 11", 72 ppgs. Retail Price: $9.99**

Geology of the Couer D'Alene Mining District of Idaho - Unavailable since 1961, this publication was originally compiled by the Idaho Bureau of Mines and Geology and includes details on the mining of gold, silver and other minerals in the famous Coeur D'Alene Mining District in Northern Idaho. Included are details on the early history of the Coeur D'Alene Mining District, local tectonic settings, ore deposit features, information on the mineral belts of the Osburn Fault, as well as detailed information on the famous Bunker Hill Mine, the Dayrock Mine, Galena Mine, Lucky Friday Mine and the infamous Sunshine Mine. This volume also includes sixteen hard to find maps. **8.5" X 11", 70 ppgs. Retail Price: $9.99**

The Gold Camps and Silver Cities of Idaho - Originally published in 1963, this important publication on Idaho Mining has not been available for nearly fifty years. Included are rare insights into the history of Idaho's Gold Rush, as well as the mad craze for silver in the Idaho Panhandle. Documented in fine detail are the early mining excitements at Boise Basin, at South Boise, in the Owyhees, at Deadwood, Long Valley, Stanley Basin and Robinson Bar, at Atlanta, on the famous Boise River, Volcano, Little Smokey, Banner, Boise Ridge, Hailey, Leesburg, Lemhi, Pearl, at South Mountain, Shoup and Ulysses, Yellow Jacket and Loon Creek. The story follows with the appearance of Chinese miners at the new mining camps on the Snake River, Black Pine, Yankee Fork, Bay Horse, Clayton, Heath, Seven Devils, Gibbonsville, Vienna and Sawtooth City. Also included are special sections on the Idaho Lead and Silver mines of the late 1800's, as well as the mining discoveries of the early 1900's that paved the way for Idaho's modern mining and mineral industry. Lavishly illustrated with rare historic photos, this volume provides a one of a kind documentary into Idaho's mining history that is sure to be enjoyed by not only modern miners and prospectors who still scour the hills in search of nature's treasures, but also those enjoy history and tromping through overgrown ghost towns and long abandoned mining camps. **8.5" X 11", 186 ppgs. Retail Price: $14.99**

Ore Deposits and Mining in North Western Custer County Idaho - Unavailable since 1913, this important publication was originally published by the Us Department of the Interior and has been unavailable for a century. Included are fine details on the geology, geography, gold placers and gold and silver bearing quartz veins of the mining region of North West Custer County, Idaho. Of particular interest is a rare look at the mines and prospects of the region, including those such as the Ramshorn Mine, SkyLark, Riverview, Excelsior, Beardsley, Pacific, Hoosier, Silver Brick, Forest Rose and dozens of others in the Bay Horse Mining District. Also covered are the mines of the Yankee Fork District such as the Lucky Boy, Badger, Black, Enterprise, Charles Dickens, Morrison, Golden Sunbeam, Montana, Golden Gate and others, as well as those in the Loon Mining District. **8.5" X 11", 126 ppgs. Retail Price: $12.99**

Gold Rush To Idaho - Unavailable since 1963, this important publication was originally published by the Idaho Bureau of Mines and has been unavailable for 50 years. "Gold Rush To Idaho" revisits the earliest years of the discovery of gold in Idaho Territory and introduces us to the conditions that the pioneer gold seekers met when they blazed a trail through the wilderness of Idaho's mountains and discovered the precious yellow metal at Oro Fino and Pierce. Subsequent rushes followed at places like Elk City, Newsome, Clearwater Station, Florence, Warrens and elsewhere. Of particular interest is a rare look at the hardships that the first miners in Idaho met with during their day to day existences and their attempts to bring law and order to their mining camps. **8.5" X 11", 88 ppgs. Retail Price: $9.99**

The Geology and Mines of Northern Idaho and North Western Montana - Unavailable since 1909, this important publication was originally published by the Us Department of the Interior and has been unavailable for a century. Included are fine details on the geology and geography of the mining regions of Northern Idaho and North Western Montana. Of particular interest is a rare look at the mines and prospects of the region, including those in the Pine Creek Mining District, Lake Pend Oreille district, Troy Mining District, Sylvanite District, Cabinet Mining District, Prospect Mining District and the Missoula Valley. Some of the mines featured include the Iron Mountain, Silver Butte, Snowshoe, Grouse Mountain Mine and others. **8.5" X 11", 142 ppgs. Retail Price: $12.99**

Mining in the Alturas Quadrangle of Blaine County Idaho - Unavailable since 1922, this important publication was originally published by the Idaho Bureau of Mines and has been unavailable for ninety years. Topics include the geology, rock formations and the formation of ore deposits in this important mining area of Idaho. Of particular focus is information on the local geology, quartz veins and ore deposits of this portion of Idaho. Included are hard to find details, including the descriptions and locations of numerous gold and silver mines in the area including the Silver King, Pilgrim, Columbia, Lone Jack, Sunbeam, Pride of the West, Lucky Boy, Scotia, Atlanta, Beaver-Bidwell and others mines and prospects. **8.5" X 11", 56 ppgs. Retail Price: $8.99**

Mining in Lemhi County Idaho - Originally published in 1913, this important book on Idaho Mining has not been available to miners for over a century. Included are rare insights into hundreds of gold, silver, copper and other mines in this famous Idaho mining area. Details include the locations, geology, history, production and other facts of the mines of this region, not only gold and silver hardrock mines, but also gold placer mines, lead-silver deposits, copper mines, cobalt-nickel deposits, tungsten and tin mines . It is lavishly illustrated with hard to find photos of the period and rare mining maps. Some of the vicinities featured include the Nicholia Mining District, Spring Mountain District, Texas District, Blue Wing District, Junction District, McDevitt District, Pratt Creek, Eldorado District, Kirtley Creek, Carmen Creek, Gibbonsville, Indian Creek, Mineral Hill District, Mackinaw, Eureka District, Blackbird District, YellowJacket District, Gravel Range District, Junction District, Parker Mountain and other mining districts. **8.5" X 11", 226 ppgs. Retail Price: $19.99**

Utah Mining Books

Fluorite in Utah - Unavailable since 1954, this publication was originally compiled by the USGS, State of Utah and U.S. Atomic Energy Commission and details the mining of fluorspar, also known as fluorite in the State of Utah. Included are details on the geology and history of fluorspar (fluorite) mining in Utah, including details on where this unique gem mineral may be found in the State of Utah. **8.5" X 11", 60 ppgs. Retail Price: $8.99**

California Mining Books

The Tertiary Gravels of the Sierra Nevada of California - Mining historian Kerby Jackson introduces us to a classic mining work by Waldemar Lindgren in this important re-issue of The Tertiary Gravels of the Sierra Nevada of California. Unavailable since 1911, this publication includes details on the gold bearing ancient river channels of the famous Sierra Nevada region of California. **8.5" X 11", 282 ppgs. Retail Price: $19.99**

The Mother Lode Mining Region of California - Unavailable since 1900, this publication includes details on the gold mines of California's famous Mother Lode gold mining area. Included are details on the geology, history and important gold mines of the region, as well as insights into historic mining methods, mine timbering, mining machinery, mining bell signals and other details on how these mines operated. Also included are insights into the gold mines of the California Mother Lode that were in operation during the first sixty years of California's mining history. **8.5" X 11", 176 ppgs. Retail Price: $14.99**

Lode Gold of the Klamath Mountains of Northern California and South West Oregon - Unavailable since 1971, this publication was originally compiled by Preston E. Hotz and includes details on the lode mining districts of Oregon and California's Klamath Mountains. Included are details on the geology, history and important lode mines of the French Gulch, Deadwood, Whiskeytown, Shasta, Redding, Muletown, South Fork, Old Diggings, Dog Creek (Delta), Bully Choop (Indian Creek), Harrison Gulch, Hayfork, Minersville, Trinity Center, Canyon Creek, East Fork, New River, Denny, Liberty (Black Bear), Cecilville, Callahan, Yreka, Fort Jones and Happy Camp mining districts in California, as well as the Ashland, Rogue River, Applegate, Illinois River, Takilma, Greenback, Galice, Silver Peak, Myrtle Creek and Mule Creek districts of South Western Oregon. Also included are insights into the mineralization and other characteristics of this important mining region. **8.5" X 11", 100 ppgs. Retail Price: $10.99**

Mines and Mineral Resources of Shasta County, Siskiyou County, Trinity County: California - Unavailable since 1915, this publication was originally compiled by the California State Mining Bureau and includes details on the gold mines of this area of Northern California. Also included are insights into the mineralization and other characteristics of this important mining region, as well as the location of historic gold mines. **8.5" X 11", 204 ppgs. Retail Price: $19.99**

Geology of the Yreka Quadrangle, Siskiyou County, California - Unavailable since 1977, this publication was originally compiled by Preston E. Hotz and includes details on the geology of the Yreka Quadrangle of Siskiyou County, California. Also included are insights into the mineralization and other characteristics of this important mining region. **8.5" X 11", 78 ppgs. Retail Price: $7.99**

Mines of San Diego and Imperial Counties, California - Originally published in 1914, this important publication on California Mining has not been available for a century. This publication includes important information on the early gold mines of San Diego and Imperial County, which were some of the first gold fields mined in California by early Spanish and Mexican miners before the 49ers came on the scene. Included are not only details on early mining methods in the area, production statistics and geological information, but also the location of the early gold mines that helped make California "The Golden State". Also included are details on the mining of other minerals such as silver, lead, zinc, manganese, tungsten, vanadium, asbestos, barite, borax, cement, clay, dolomite, fluospar, gem stones, graphite, marble, salines, petroleum, stronium, talc and others. **8.5" X 11", 116 ppgs. Retail Price: $12.99**

Mines of Sierra County, California - Unavailable since 1920, this publication was originally compiled by the California State Mining Bureau and includes details on the gold mines of Sierra County, California. Also included are insights into the mineralization and other characteristics of this important mining region, as well as the location of historic gold mines. **8.5" X 11", 156 ppgs. Retail Price: $19.99**

Mines of Plumas County, California - Unavailable since 1918, this publication was originally compiled by the California State Mining Bureau and includes details on the gold mines of Plumas County, California. Also included are insights into the mineralization and other characteristics of this important mining region, as well as the location of historic gold mines. **8.5" X 11", 200 ppgs. Retail Price: $19.99**

Mines of El Dorado, Placer, Sacramento and Yuba Counties, California - Originally published in 1917, this important publication on California Mining has not been available for nearly a century. This publication includes important information on the early gold mines of El Dorado County, Placer County, Sacramento County and Yuba County, which were some of the first gold fields mined by the Forty-Niners during the California Gold Rush. Included are not only details on early mining methods in the area, production statistics and geological information, but also the location of the early gold mines that helped make California "The Golden State". Also included are insights into the early mining of chrome, copper and other minerals in this important mining area. **8.5" X 11", 204 ppgs. Retail Price: $19.99**

Mines of Los Angeles, Orange and Riverside Counties, California - Originally published in 1917, this important publication on California Mining has not been available for nearly a century. This publication includes important information on the early gold mines of Los Angeles County, Orange County and Riverside County, which were some of the first gold fields mined in California by early Spanish and Mexican miners before the 49ers came on the scene. Included are not only details on early mining methods in the area, production statistics and geological information, but also the location of the early gold mines that helped make California "The Golden State". **8.5" X 11", 146 ppgs. Retail Price: $12.99**

Mines of San Bernadino and Tulare Counties, California - Originally published in 1917, this important publication on California Mining has not been available for nearly a century. This publication includes important information on the early gold mines of San Bernadino and Tulare County, which were some of the first gold fields mined in California by early Spanish and Mexican miners before the 49ers came on the scene. Included are not only details on early mining methods in the area, production statistics and geological information, but also the location of the early gold mines that helped make California "The Golden State". Also included are details on the mining of other minerals such as copper, iron, lead, zinc, manganese, tungsten, vanadium, asbestos, barite, borax, cement, clay, dolomite, fluospar, gem stones, graphite, marble, salines, petroleum, stronium, talc and others. **8.5" X 11", 200 ppgs. Retail Price: $19.99**

Chromite Mining in The Klamath Mountains of California and Oregon - Unavailable since 1919, this publication was originally compiled by J.S. Diller of the United States Department of Geological Survey and includes details on the chromite mines of this area of Northern California and Southern Oregon. Also included are insights into the mineralization and other characteristics of this important mining region, as well as the location of historic mines. Also included are insights into chromite mining in Eastern Oregon and Montana. **8.5" X 11", 98 ppgs. Retail Price: $9.99**

Mines and Mining in Amador, Calaveras and Tuolumne Counties, California - Unavailable since 1915, this publication was originally compiled by William Tucker and includes details on the mines and mineral resources of this important California mining area. Included are details on the geology, history and important gold mines of the region, as well as insights into other local mineral resources such as asbestos, clay, copper, talc, limestone and others. Also included are insights into the mineralization and other characteristics of this important portion of California's Mother Lode mining region. 8.5" X 11", 198 ppgs. Retail Price: $14.99

The Cerro Gordo Mining District of Inyo County California - Unavailable since 1963, this publication was originally compiled by the United States Department of Interior. Included are insights into the mineralization and other characteristics of this important mining region of Southern California. Topics include the mining of gold and silver in this important mining district in Inyo County, California, including details on the history, production and locations of the Cerro Gordo Mine, the Morning Star Mine, Estelle Tunnel, Charles Lease Tunnel, Ignacio, Hart, Crosscut Tunnel, Sunset, Upper Newtown, Newtown, Ella, Perseverance, Newsboy, Belmont and other silver and gold mines in the Cerro Gordo Mining District. This volume also includes important insights into the fossil record, geologic formations, faults and other aspects of economic geology in this California mining district. 8.5" X 11", 104 ppgs. Retail Price: $10.99

Mining in Butte, Lassen, Modoc, Sutter and Tehama Counties of California - Unavailable since 1917, this publication was originally compiled by the United States Department of Interior. Included are insights into the mineralization and other characteristics of this important mining region of California. Topics include the mining of asbestos, chromite, gold, diamonds and manganese in Butte County, the mining of gold and copper in the Hayden Hill and Diamond Mountain mining districts of Lassen County, the mining of coal, salt, copper and gold in the High Grade and Winters mining districts of Modoc County, gold mining in Sutter County and the mining of gold, chromite, manganese and copper in Tehama County. This volume also includes the production records and locations of numerous mines in this important mining region. 8.5" X 11", 114 ppgs. Retail Price: $11.99

Mines of Trinity County California - Originally published in 1965, this important publication on California Mining has not been available for nearly fifty years. This publication includes important information on mines and mining in Trinity County, California, as well insights into the mineralization and geology of this important mining area in Northern California. Included are extensive details on hardrock and placer gold mines and prospects, including charts showing the locations of these historic mines.. 8.5" X 11", 144 ppgs. Retail Price: $12.99

Mines of Kern County California - Originally published in 1962, this important publication on California Mining has not been available for nearly fifty years. This publication includes important information on mines and mining in Kern County, California, as well insights into the mineralization and geology of this important mining area in California. Included are extensive details on hardrock and placer gold mines and prospects, including charts showing the locations of these historic mines. 8.5" X 11", 398 ppgs. Retail Price: $24.99

Mines of Calaveras County California - Originally published in 1962, this important publication on California Mining has not been available for nearly fifty years. This publication includes important information on mines and mining in Calaveras County, California, as well insights into the mineralization and geology of this important mining area in Northern California. Included are extensive details on hardrock and placer gold mines and prospects, including charts showing the locations of these historic mines. 8.5" X 11", 236 ppgs. Retail Price: $19.99

Lode Gold Mining in Grass Valley California - Unavailable since 1940, this publication was originally compiled by the United States Department of Interior. Included are insights into the gold mineralization and other characteristics of this important mining region of Nevada County, California. This volume also includes important insights into the geologic formations, faults and other aspects of economic geology in this California mining district. Of particular interest are the fine details on many hardrock gold mines in the area, including their locations, histories, development and mineralization. Some of the mines featured include the Gold Hill Mine, Massachusetts Hill, Boundary, Peabody, Golden Center, North Star, Omaha, Lone Jack, Homeward Bound, Hartery, Wisconsin, Allison Ranch, Phoenix, Kate Hayes, W.Y.O.D., Empire, Rich Hill, Daisy Hill, Orleans, Sultana, Centennial, Conlin, Ben Franklin, Crown Point and many others. 8.5" X 11", 148 ppgs. Retail Price: $12.99

Lode Mining in the Alleghany District of Sierra County California - Unavailable since 1913, this publication was originally compiled by the United States Department of Interior. Included are insights into the mineralization and other characteristics of this important mining region of Sierra County. Included are details on the history, production and locations of numerous hardrock gold mines in this famous California area, including the Tightner Mine, Minnie D., Osceola, Eldorado, Twenty One, Sherman, Kenton, Oriental, Rainbow, Plumbago, Irelan, Gold Canyon, North Fork, Federal, Kate Hardy and others. This volume also includes important insights into the fossil record, geologic formations, faults and other aspects of economic geology in this California mining district. 8.5" X 11", 48 ppgs. Retail Price: $7.99

Six Months In The Gold Mines During The California Gold Rush - Unavailable since 1850, this important work is a first hand account of one "49'ers" personal experience during the great California Gold Rush, shedding important light on one of the most exciting periods in the history of not only California, but also the world. Compiled from journals written between 1847 and 1849 by E. Gould Buffum, a native of New York, "Six Months In The Gold Mines During The California Gold Rush" offers a rare look into the day to day lives of the people who came to California to work in her gold mines when the state was still a great frontier. 8.5" X 11", 290 ppgs. Retail Price: $19.99

Quartz Mines of the Grass Valley Mining District of California - Unavailable since 1867, this important publication has not been available since those days. This rare publication offers a short dissertation on the early hardrock mines in this important mining district in the California Mother Lode region between the 1850's and 1860's. Also included are hard to find details on the mineralization and locations of these mines, as well as how they were operated in those day. 8.5" X 11", 44 ppgs. Retail Price: $8.99

Alaska Mining Books

Ore Deposits of the Willow Creek Mining District, Alaska - Unavailable since 1954, this hard to find publication includes valuable insights into the Willow Creek Mining District near Hatcher Pass in Alaska. The publication includes insights into the history, geology and locations of the well known mines in the area, including the Gold Cord, Independence, Fern, Mabel, Lonesome, Snowbird, Schroff-O'Neil, High Grade, Marion Twin, Thorpe, Webfoot, Kelly-Willow, Lane, Holland and others. 8.5" X 11", 96 ppgs. Retail Price: $9.99

The Juneau Gold Belt of Alaska - Unavailable since 1906, this hard to find publication includes valuable insights into the gold mines around Juneau, Alaska. The publication includes important details into the history, geology and locations of the well known gold mines and prospects in the area, including those around Windham Bay, Holkham Bay, Port Snettisham, on Grindstone and Rhine Creeks, Gold Creek, Douglas Island, Salmon Creek, Lemon Creek, Nugget Creek, from the Mendenhall River to Berners Bay, McGinnis Creek, Montana Creek, Peterson Creek, Windfall Creek, the Eagle River, Yankee Basin, Yankee Curve, Kowee Creek and elsewhere. Not only are gold placer mines included, but also hardrock gold mines. 8.5" X 11", 224 ppgs. Retail Price: $19.99

Arizona Mining Books

Mines and Mining in Northern Yuma County Arizona - Originally published in 1911, this important publication on Arizona Mining has not been available for over a hundred years. Included are rare insights into the gold, silver, copper and quicksilver mines of Yuma County, Arizona together with hard to find maps and photographs. Some of the mines and mining districts featured include the Planet Copper Mine, Mineral Hill, the Clara Consolidated Mine, Viati Mine, Copper Basin prospect, Bowman Mine, Quartz King, Billy Mack, Carnation, the Wardwell and Osbourne, Valensuella Copper, the Mariquita, Colonial Mine, the French American, the New York-Plomosa, Guadalupe, Lead Camp, Mudersbach Copper Camp, Yellow Bird, the Arizona Northern (Salome Strike), Bonanza (Harqua Hala), Golden Eagle, Hercules, Socorro and others. 8.5" X 11", 144 ppgs. Retail Price: $11.99

The Aravaipa and Stanley Mining Districts of Graham County Arizona - Originally published in 1925, this important publication on Arizona Mining has not been available for nearly ninety years. Included are rare insights into the gold and silver mines of these two important mining districts, together with hard to find maps. 8.5" X 11", 140 ppgs. Retail Price: $11.99

Gold in the Gold Basin and Lost Basin Mining Districts of Mohave County, Arizona - This volume contains rare insights into the geology and gold mineralization of the Gold Basin and Lost Basin Mining Districts of Mohave County, Arizona that will be of benefit to miners and prospectors. Also included is a significant body of information on the gold mines and prospects of this portion of Arizona. This volume is lavishly illustrated with rare photos and mining maps. 8.5" X 11", 188 ppgs. Retail Price: $19.99

Mines of the Jerome and Bradshaw Mountains of Arizona - This important publication on Arizona Mining has not been available for ninety years. This volume contains rare insights into the geology and ore deposits of the Jerome and Bradshaw Mountains of Arizona that will be of benefit to miners and prospectors who work those areas. Included is a significant body of information on the mines and prospects of the Verde, Black Hills, Cherry Creek, Prescott, Walker, Groom Creek, Hassayampa, Bigbug, Turkey Creek, Agua Fria, Black Canyon, Peck, Tiger, Pine Grove, Bradshaw, Tintop, Humbug and Castle Creek Mining Districts. This volume is lavishly illustrated with rare photos and mining maps. 8.5" X 11", 218 ppgs. Retail Price: $19.99

The Ajo Mining District of Pima County Arizona - This important publication on Arizona Mining has not been available for nearly seventy years. This volume contains rare insights into the geology and mineralization of the Ajo Mining District in Pima County, Arizona and in particular the famous New Cornelia Mine. 8.5" X 11", 126 ppgs. Retail Price: $11.99

Mining in the Santa Rita and Patagonia Mountains of Arizona - Originally published in 1915, this important publication on Arizona Mining has not been available for nearly a century. Included are rare insights into hundreds of gold, silver, copper and other mines in this famous Arizona mining area. Details include the locations, geology, history, production and other facts of the mines of this region. **8.5" X 11", 394 ppgs. Retail Price: $24.99**

Mining in the Bisbee Quadrangle of Arizona - Originally published in 1906, this important publication on Arizona Mining has not been available for nearly a century. Included are rare insights into hundreds of gold, silver, copper and other mines in this famous Arizona mining area. Details include the locations, geology, history, production and other facts of the mines of this important mining region. **8.5" X 11", 188 ppgs. Retail Price: $14.99**

Montana Mining Books

A History of Butte Montana: The World's Greatest Mining Camp - First published in 1900 by H.C. Freeman, this important publication sheds a bright light on one of the most important mining areas in the history of The West. Together with his insights, as well as rare photographs of the periods, Harry Freeman describes Butte and its vicinity from its early beginnings, right up to its flush years when copper flowed from its mines like a river. At the time of publication, Butte, Montana was known worldwide as "The Richest Mining Spot On Earth" and produced not only vast amounts of copper, but also silver, gold and other metals from its mines. Freeman illustrates, with great detail, the most important mines in the vicinity of Butte, providing rare details on their owners, their history and most importantly, how the mines operated and how their treasures were extracted. Of particular interest are the dozens of rare photographs that depict mines such as the famous Anaconda, the Silver Bow, the Smoke House, Moose, Paulin, Buffalo, Little Minah, the Mountain Consolidated, West Greyrock, Cora, the Green Mountain, Diamond, Bell, Parnell, the Neversweat, Nipper, Original and many others. **8.5" X 11", 142 ppgs. Retail Price: $12.99**

The Butte Mining District of Montana - This important publication on Montana Mining has not been available for over a century. Included are rare insights into the gold, copper and silver mines of Butte, Montana together with hard to find maps and photographs. Some of the topics include the early history of gold, silver and copper mining in the Butte area, insight into the geology of its mining areas, the local distribution of gold, silver and copper ores, as well their composition and how to identify them. Also included are detailed facts about the mines in the Butte Mining District, including the famous Anaconda Mine, Gagnon, Parrot, Blue Vein, Moscow, Poulin, Stella, Buffalo, Green Mountain, Wake Up Jim, the Diamond-Bell Group, Mountain Consolidated, East Greyrock, West Greyrock, Snowball, Corra, Speculator, Adirondack, Miners Union, the Jessie-Edith May Group, Otisco, Iduna, Colorado, Lizzie, Cambers, Anderson, Hesperus, Preferencia and dozens of others. **8.5" X 11", 298 ppgs. Retail Price: $24.99**

Mines of the Helena Mining Region of Montana - This important publication on Montana Mining has not been available for over a century. Included are rare insights into the gold, copper and silver mines of the vicinity of Helena, Montana, including the Marysville Mining District, Elliston Mining District, Rimini Mining District, Helena Mining District, Clancy Mining District, Wickes Mining District, Boulder and Basin Mining Districts and the Elkhorn Mining District. Some of the topics include the early history of gold, silver and copper mining in the Helena area, insight into the geology of its mining areas, the local distribution of gold, silver and copper ores, as well their composition and how to identify them. Also included are detailed facts, history, geology and locations of over one hundred gold, silver and copper mines in the area . **8.5" X 11", 162 ppgs, Retail Price: $14.99**

Mines and Geology of the Garnet Range of Montana - This important publication on Montana Mining has not been available for over a century. Included are rare insights into the gold, copper and silver mines of the vicinity of this important mining area of Montana. Some of the topics include the early history of gold, silver and copper mining in the Garnet Mountains, insight into the geology of its mining areas, the local distribution of gold, silver and copper ores, as well their composition and how to identify them. Also included are detailed facts, history, geology and locations of numerous gold, silver and copper mines in the area . **8.5" X 11", 100 ppgs, Retail Price: $11.99**

Mines and Geology of the Philipsburg Quadrangle of Montana - This important publication on Montana Mining has not been available for over a century. Included are rare insights into the gold, copper and silver mines of the vicinity of this important mining area of Montana. Some of the topics include the early history of gold, silver and copper mining in the Philipsburg Quadrangle, insight into the geology of its mining areas, the local distribution of gold, silver and copper ores, as well their composition and how to identify them. Also included are detailed facts, history, geology and locations of over one hundred gold, silver and copper mines in the area **8.5" X 11", 290 ppgs, Retail Price: $24.99**

Geology of the Marysville Mining District of Montana - Included are rare insights into the mining geology of the Marysville Mining District. Some of the topics include the early history of gold, silver and copper mining in the area, insight into the geology of its mining areas, the local distribution of gold, silver and copper ores, as well their composition and how to identify them. Also included are detailed facts, history, geology and locations of gold, silver and copper mines in the area **8.5" X 11", 198 ppgs, Retail Price: $19.99**

<u>The Geology and Mines of Northern Idaho and North Western Montana</u>

See listing under Idaho.

Nevada Mining Books

<u>The Bull Frog Mining District of Nevada</u> - Unavailable since 1910, this publication was originally compiled by the United States Department of Interior. This volume also includes important insights into the geologic formations, faults and other aspects of economic geology in this Nevada mining district. Of particular interest are the fine details on many mines in the area, including their locations, histories, development and mineralization. Some of the mines featured include the National Bank Mine, Providence, Gibraltor, Tramps, Denver, Original Bullfrog, Gold Bar, Mayflower, Homestake-King and other mines and prospects. **8.5" X 11", 152 ppgs, Retail Price: $14.99**

<u>History of the Comstock Lode</u> - Unavailable since 1876, this publication was originally released by John Wiley & Sons. This volume also includes important insights into the famous Comstock Lode of Nevada that represented the first major silver discovery in the United States. During its spectacular run, the Comstock produced over 192 million ounces of silver and 8.2 million ounces of gold. Not only did the Comstock result in one of the largest mining rushes in history and yield immense fortunes for its owners, but it made important contributions to the development of the State of Nevada, as well as neighboring California. Included here are important details on not only the early development and history of the Comstock, but also rare early insight into its mines, ore and its geology.**8.5" X 11", 244 ppgs, Retail Price: $19.99**

Colorado Mining Books

<u>Ores of The Leadville Mining District</u> - Unavailable since 1926, this publication was originally compiled by the United States Department of Interior. This volume also includes important insights into the ores and mineralization of the Leadville Mining District in Colorado. Topics include historic ore prospecting methods, local geology, insights into ore veins and stockworks, the local trend and distribution of ore channels, reverse faults, shattered rock above replacement ore bodies, mineral enrichment in oxidized and sulphide zones and more. **8.5" X 11", 66 ppgs, Retail Price: $8.99**

<u>Mining in Colorado</u> - Unavailable since 1926, this publication was originally compiled by the United States Department of Interior. This volume also includes important insights into the mining history of Colorado from its early beginnings in the 1850's right up to the mid 1920's. Not only is Colorado's gold mining heritage included, but also its silver, copper, lead and zinc mining industry. Each mining area is treated separately, detailing the development of Colorado's mines on a county by county basis. **8.5" X 11", 284 ppgs, Retail Price: $19.99**

<u>Gold Mining in Gilpin County Colorado</u> - Unavailable since 1876, this publication was originally compiled by the Register Steam Printing House of Central City, Colorado. A rare glimpse at the gold mining history and early mines of Gilpin County, Colorado from their first discovery in the 1850's up to the "flush years" of the mid 1870's. Of particular interest is the history of the discovery of gold in Gilpin County and details about the men who made those first strikes. Special focus is given to the early gold mines and first mining districts of the area, many of which are not detailed in other books on Colorado's gold mining history. **8.5" X 11", 156 ppgs, Retail Price: $12.99**

<u>Mining in the Gold Brick Mining District of Colorado</u> - Important insights into the history of the Gold Brick Mining District, as well as its local geography and economic geology. Also included are the histories and locations of historic mines in this important Colorado Mining District, including the Cortland, Carter, Raymond, Gold Links, Sacramento, Bassick, Sandy Hook, Chronicle, Grand Prize, Chloride, Granite Mountain, Lucille, Gray Mountain, Hilltop, Maggie Mitchell, Silver Islet, Revenue, Roosevelt, Carbonate King and others. In addition to hardrock mining, are also included are details on gold placer mining in this portion of Colorado. **8.5" X 11", 140 ppgs, Retail Price: $12.99**

Washington Mining Books

<u>The Republic Mining District of Washington</u> - Unavailable since 1910, this important publication was originally published by the Washington Geologic Survey and has been unavailable for a century. Topics include the geology, rock formations and the formation of ore deposits in this important mining area of Washington State. Also included are hard to find details on the geology, history and locations of dozens of mines in the area. Some of the mines featured include the New Republic Mine, Ben Hur, Morning Glory, the South Republic Mine, Quilp, Surprise, Black Tail, Lone Pine, San Poil, Mountain Lion, Tom Thumb, Elcaliph and many others. **8.5" X 11", 94 ppgs, Retail Price: $10.99**

Wyoming Mining Books

Mining in the Laramie Basin of Wyoming - Unavailable since 1909, this publication was originally compiled by the United States Department of Interior. Also included are insights into the mineralization and other characteristics of this important mining region, especially in regards to coal, limestone, gypsum, bentonite clay, cement, sand, clay and copper. **8.5" X 11", 104 ppgs, Retail Price: $11.99**

New Mexico Mining Books

The Mogollon Mining District of New Mexico - Unavailable since 1927, this important publication was originally published by the US Department of Interior and has been unavailable for 80 years. Topics include the geology, rock formations and the formation of ore deposits in this important mining area in New Mexico. Of particular focus is information on the history and production of the ore deposits in this area, their form and structure, vein filling, their paragenesis, origins and ore shoots, as well as oxidation and supergene enrichment. Also included are hard to find details, including the descriptions and locations of numerous gold, silver and other types of mines, including the Eureka, Pacific, South Alpine, Great Western, Enterprise, Buffalo, Mountain View, Floride, Gold Dust, Last Chance, Deadwood, Confidence, Maud S., Deep Down, Little Fanney, Trilby, Johnson, Alberta, Comet, Golden Eagle, Cooney, Queen, the Iron Crown, Eberle, Clifton, Andrew Jackson mine, Mascot and others. **8.5" X 11", 144 ppgs, Retail Price: $12.99**

The Percha Mining District of Kingston New Mexico - Unavailable since 1883, this important publication was originally published by the Kingston Tribune and has been unavailable for over one hundred and thirty five years. Having been written during the earliest years of gold and silver mining in the Percha Mining District, unlike other books on the subject, this work offers the unique perspective of having actually been written while the early mining history of this area was still being made. In fact, the work was written so early in the development of this area that many of the notable mines in the Percha District were less than a few years old and were still being operated by their original discoverers with the same enthusiasm as when they were first located. Included are hard to find details on the very earliest gold and silver mines of this important mining district near Kingston in Sierra County, New Mexico. **8.5" X 11", 68 ppgs, Retail Price: $9.99**

East Coast Mining Books

The Gold Fields of the Southern Appalachians - Unavailable since 1895, this important publication was originally published by the US Department of Interior and has been unavailable for nearly 120 years. Topics include the geology, rock formations and the formation of ore deposits in this important mining area of the American South. Of particular focus is information on the history and statistics of the ore deposits in this area, their form and structure and veins. Also included are details on the placer gold deposits of the region. The gold fields of the Georgian Belt, Carolinian Belt and the South Mountain Mining District of North Carolina are all treated in descriptive detail. Included are hard to find details, including the descriptions and locations of numerous gold mines in Georgia, North Carolina and elsewhere in the American South. Also included are details on the gold belts of the British Maritime Provinces and the Green Mountains. **8.5" X 11", 104 ppgs, Retail Price: $9.99**

Gold Rush Tales Series

Millions in Siskiyou County Gold - In this first volume of the "Gold Rush Tales" series, leading mining historian and editor Kerby Jackson, introduces us to the story of how millions of dollars worth of gold was discovered in Siskiyou County during the California Gold Rush. Lavishly illustrated with photos from the 19th Century, this hard to find information was first published in 1897 and sheds important light onto the gold rush era in Siskiyou County, California and the experiences of the men who dug for the gold and actually found it. **8.5" X 11", 82 ppgs, Retail Price: $9.99**

The California Rand in the Days of '49 - In this second volume of the "Gold Rush Tales" series, leading mining historian and editor Kerby Jackson, introduces us to four tales from the California Gold Rush. Lavishly illustrated with photos from the 19th Century, this hard to find information was first published in 1890's and includes the stories of "California's Rand", details about Chinese miners, how one early miner named Baker struck it rich and also the story of Alphonzo Bowers, who invented the first hydraulic gold dredge. **8.5" X 11", 54 ppgs, Retail Price: $9.99**

More Mining Books

Prospecting and Developing A Small Mine - Topics covered include the classification of varying ores, how to take a proper ore sample, the proper reduction of ore samples, alluvial sampling, how to understand geology as it is applied to prospecting and mining, prospecting procedures, methods of ore treatment, the application of drilling and blasting in a small mine and other topics that the small scale miner will find of benefit. **8.5" X 11", 112 ppgs, Retail Price: $11.99**

Timbering For Small Underground Mines - Topics covered include the selection of caps and posts, the treatment of mine timbers, how to install mine timbers, repairing damaged timbers, use of drift supports, headboards, squeeze sets, ore chute construction, mine cribbing, square set timbering methods, the use of steel and concrete sets and other topics that the small underground miner will find of benefit. This volume also includes twenty eight illustrations depicting the proper construction of mine timbering and support systems that greatly enhance the practical usability of the information contained in this small book. **8.5" X 11", 88 ppgs. Retail Price: $10.99**

Timbering and Mining - A classic mining publication on Hard Rock Mining by W.H. Storms. Unavailable since 1909, this rare publication provides an in depth look at American methods of underground mine timbering and mining methods. Topics include the selection and preservation of mine timbers, drifting and drift sets, driving in running ground, structural steel in mine workings, timbering drifts in gravel mines, timbering methods for driving shafts, positioning drill holes in shafts, timbering stations at shafts, drainage, mining large ore bodies by means of open cuts or by the "Glory Hole" system, stoping out ore in flat or low lying veins, use of the "Caving System", stoping in swelling ground, how to stope out large ore bodies, Square Set timbering on the Comstock and its modifications by California miners, the construction of ore chutes, stoping ore bodies by use of the "Block System", how to work dangerous ground, information on the "Delprat System" of stoping without mine timbers, construction and use of headframes and much more. This volume provides a reference into not only practical methods of mining and timbering that may be employed in narrow vein mining by small miners today, but also rare insights into how mines were being worked at the turn of the 19th Century. **8.5" X 11", 288 ppgs. Retail Price: $24.99**

A Study of Ore Deposits For The Practical Miner - Mining historian Kerby Jackson introduces us to a classic mining publication on ore deposits by J.P. Wallace. First published in 1908, it has been unavailable for over a century. Included are important insights into the properties of minerals and their identification, on the occurrence and origin of gold, on gold alloys, insights into gold bearing sulfides such as pyrites and arsenopyrites, on gold bearing vanadium, gold and silver tellurides, lead and mercury tellurides, on silver ores, platinum and iridium, mercury ores, copper ores, lead ores, zinc ores, iron ores, chromium ores, manganese ores, nickel ores, tin ores, tungsten ores and others. Also included are facts regarding rock forming minerals, their composition and occurrences, on igneous, sedimentary, metamorphic and intrusive rocks, as well as how they are geologically disturbed by dikes, flows and faults, as well as the effects of these geologic actions and why they are important to the miner. Written specifically with the common miner and prospector in mind, the book will help to unlock the earth's hidden wealth for you and is written in a simple and concise language that anyone can understand. **8.5" X 11", 366 ppgs. Retail Price: $24.99**

Mine Drainage - Unavailable since 1896, this rare publication provides an in depth look at American methods of underground mine drainage and mining pump systems. This volume provides a reference into not only practical methods of mining drainage that may be employed in narrow vein mining by small miners today, but also rare insights into how mines were being worked at the turn of the 19th Century. **8.5" X 11", 218 ppgs. Retail Price: $24.99**

Fire Assaying Gold, Silver and Lead Ores - Unavailable since 1907, this important publication was originally published by the Mining and Scientific Press and was designed to introduce miners and prospectors of gold, silver and lead to the art of fire assaying. Topics include the fire assaying of ores and products containing gold, silver and lead; the sampling and preparation of ore for an assay; care of the assay office, assay furnaces; crucibles and scorifiers; assay balances; metallic ores; scorification assays; cupelling; parting' crucible assays, the roasting of ores and more. This classic provides a time honored method of assaying put forward in a clear, concise and easy to understand language that will make it a benefit to even beginners. **8.5" X 11", 96 ppgs. Retail Price: $11.99**

Methods of Mine Timbering - Originally published in 1896, this important publication on mining engineering has not been available for nearly a century. Included are rare insights into historical methods of timbering structural support that were used in underground metal mines during the California that still have a practical application for the small scale hardrock miner of today. **8.5" X 11", 94 ppgs. Retail Price: $10.99**

The Enrichment of Copper Sulfide Ores - First published in 1913, it has been unavailable for over a century. Topics include the definition and types of ore enrichment, the oxidation of copper ores, the precipitation of metallic sulfides. Also included are the results of dozens of lab experiments pertaining to the enrichment of sulfide ores that will be of interest to the practical hard rock mine operator in his efforts to release the metallic bounty from his mine's ore. **8.5" X 11", 92 ppgs. Retail Price: $9.99**

A Study of Magmatic Sulfide Ores - Unavailable since 1914, this rare publication provides an in depth look at magmatic sulfide ores. Some of the topics included are the definition and classification of magmatic ores, descriptions of some magmatic sulfide ore deposits known at the time of publication including copper and nickel bearing pyrrhitic ore bodies, chalcopyrite-bornite deposits, pyritic deposits, magnetite-ileminite deposits, chromite deposits and magmatic iron ore deposits. Also included are details on how to recognize these types of ore deposits while prospecting for valuable hardrock minerals. **8.5" X 11", 138 ppgs. Retail Price: $11.99**

<u>The Cyanide Process of Gold Recovery</u> - Unavailable since 1894 and released under the name "The Cyanide Process: Its Practical Application and Economical Results", this rare publication provides an in depth look at the early use of cyanide leaching for gold recovery from hardrock mine ores. This volume provides a reference into the early development and use of cyanide leaching to recover gold. **8.5" X 11", 162 ppgs. Retail Price: $14.99**

<u>California Gold Milling Practices</u> - Unavailable since 1895 and released under the name "California Gold Practices", this rare publication provides an in depth look at early methods of milling used to reduce gold ores in California during the late 19th century. This volume provides a reference into the early development and use of milling equipment during the earliest years of the California Gold Rush up to the age of the Industrial Revolution. Much of the information still applies today and will be of use to small scale miners engaging in hardrock mining. **8.5" X 11", 104 ppgs. Retail Price: $10.99**

Made in United States
Troutdale, OR
09/11/2023